To Katie
Merry Christmas
& Miracles Always!
Kris

I Witness News.
I Witness Miracles:
A Reporter's Notebook

GOOD THINGS ARE HAPPENING IN YOUR LIFE EVERY DAY. LEARN HOW
TO OPEN YOUR EYES AND YOUR HEART TO A HAPPIER WAY OF LIFE.

Kris Patrow

BALBOA.
PRESS

A DIVISION OF HAY HOUSE

Balboa Press books may be ordered through booksellers or by contacting:

Balboa Press
A Division of Hay House
1663 Liberty Drive
Bloomington, IN 47403
www.balboapress.com
1-(877) 407-4847

Because of the dynamic nature of the Internet, any web addresses or links contained in
this book may have changed since publication and may no longer be valid. The views
expressed in this work are solely those of the author and do not necessarily reflect the
views of the publisher, and the publisher hereby disclaims any responsibility for them.

The author of this book does not dispense medical advice or prescribe the use of any
technique as a form of treatment for physical, emotional, or medical problems without the
advice of a physician, either directly or indirectly. The intent of the author is only to offer
information of a general nature to help you in your quest for emotional and spiritual well-
being. In the event you use any of the information in this book for yourself, which is your
constitutional right, the author and the publisher assume no responsibility for your actions.

Any people depicted in stock imagery provided by Thinkstock are models,
and such images are being used for illustrative purposes only.
Certain stock imagery © Thinkstock.

ISBN: 978-1-4525-3975-1 (sc)
ISBN: 978-1-4525-3976-8 (dj)
ISBN: 978-1-4525-3974-4 (e)

Library of Congress Control Number: 2011917033

Printed in the United States of America

Balboa Press rev. date: 10/26/2011

To Dave, my life's love.
Thank you for the many miracles
you've given me—and continue to give me—every day.
I love you.

Contents

Preface

I've got good news and bad news.

The bad news is, well ... that there is a lot of bad news out there. At least if you're getting it from TV. Eighty-three percent of Americans believe that television news is the most negative, as compared to newspapers, radio, and the Internet (*The Wirthlin Report*, February 2004). That's partly my fault. For nearly twenty years I was one of the people bringing it into your living room. I was a television news anchor and reporter. Bad news was my job.

The good news is ... that's not the whole story. It never was. And I'm on a mission to prove it. *I Witness News. I Witness Miracles: A Reporter's Notebook* is step one of that mission: from reporting the countless "good news" stories that never made air, to pointing out the good things that happen in everyday life; things that many people have forgotten how to see in this gloom-and-doom world painted by the media.

Even though 51 percent of all US adults watch local TV news at least seven times a week (Gallup Poll, December 2008), only 9 percent say they have a great deal of trust that the mass media reports the news fully, accurately, and fairly (Gallup Poll, September 2008). That means at least 91 percent believe that today's TV news is "missing something." Part of that "something," in my experience, is the good news that doesn't make the headlines—the very news that *I Witness News. I Witness Miracles: A Reporter's Notebook* is all about.

I've reported on neglected orphans in Romania, children with heart defects in Colombia whose families couldn't afford life-saving surgery, and Midwestern communities devastated by tornadoes. From

ix

my years producing programs for CNBC and the Discovery Channel, to those reporting for several network affiliates, the stories shared a common thread. Although the assignments and the people involved were different, miracles ultimately showed up before all hope was lost.

At a time when television news has many of us closing our doors and eyeing each other with suspicion, *I Witness News. I Witness Miracles: A Reporter's Notebook* reports stories that will help people to see each other and the world in a new, more compassionate way; to "see" miracles so common they re-thread the needle connecting us to one another.

Introduction

It all began when …

I was in second grade.

I had this teacher, Miss Brunner. She seemed to be about 103. Her hair was the color and consistency of spun glass, and it was always curled "just so," up and away from her face so that it seemed to pull her whole face back into a smile. I remember she had really big teeth. Not scary teeth, like a bear or anything. Just big, smiling horse teeth. And she smiled so much that there were permanent parentheses around her mouth and eyes. She wore thick granny glasses too. The kind that made her eyes look gigantic. But even those big eyes were always smiling. From the first day I saw her, I knew she must be a nice lady.

And she was, except for the fact that she was a stickler for us kids being able to write well. Not just the horrifying contortions required for cursive writing, but also the imagination for *creative* cursive writing. I was lucky. My mom had been an English major in college. Plus, she was a librarian, so she was big on my being able to read and write well too. Mom was really good at writing corny poems for friends and family events. So I tried my hand at some creative, corny poems and found out that I had, in fact, inherited my mother's gene for them. I thought they were fun, figuring out words that sounded the same. I made birthday cards and Father's Day cards and poems about Grandma's crazy cat, Dusty. Then I started writing about more "serious" topics: how much I loved horses; how I loved the changing seasons; and how cool it was that Christmas had both the new baby Jesus and the present-bringing Santa to get excited about.

It was the latter kind of poems (the un-corny ones) that Miss Brunner about smiled her head off over. She encouraged me to submit some of my writing to a book called *Creative Voices,* a collection of grade school kids' poems and short stories published once a year. And two of my poems made it. I was *so* excited! Published by age nine. I was as full of myself as I could be at that age. Until Miss Brunner uttered the words I'd never forget. It was at my parent-teacher conference. I heard her say to my mom, "I'm not going to die until Kris publishes her first book." I was horrified. First, I didn't *ever* want Miss Brunner to die, so that made me *not* want to write a book *ever*. But then again, I didn't want to make the poor woman suffer. After all, she was already 103 by my estimates, and I couldn't imagine her going blind and deaf and getting all arthritic, all the while refusing to die peacefully because I hadn't been published yet.

I vowed that someday I would write that book. Then I got on with the business of being nine.

Well, it's 38 years later. Thirty-eight years of Miss Brunner "hanging around" (even though she did die eventually), waiting for me to go ahead and write this book. She's still smiling. And sometimes I think I can "feel" her bony hand on my shoulder, her knuckles all big and gnarled, but with skin and a touch as soft as parchment. She's waiting, poor soul ... but she believes in me and has all these years.

So, dammit, here I am, writing my book, *I Witness News. I Witness Miracles: A Reporter's Notebook*—partly because of an old teacher I consider to be one of those miracles. Rest in peace, Miss Brunner. Here goes ...

My dream job: getting ready to do a live report for KSTP-TV

"When I grow up, I want to be ...

"A television news reporter." I can't count how many times I said that. I said it so many times that when I finally did land my dream job in news at age 30, my mother simply said, "Thank God!" so she wouldn't have to hear about it anymore.

And I loved it. I loved writing. I loved the excitement of being right where the news was when it was happening. I traveled the world, and I got to meet famous people. And I got to be on TV, which I have to admit is pretty cool—unless you're standing outside in minus-fifty-degree weather, telling people they shouldn't go outside. Then you just feel like an idiot.

Anyway, not long into my career, it started to bother me that the only news we seemed to tell was *bad* news, even if something good was going on behind the scenes in the same story. Like the tow-truck driver in Spencer, South Dakota who helped pull his neighbors' cars and tractors from the rubble after a devastating tornado, even though his own home and all of his belongings had been destroyed. Wouldn't you want to hear about something like that? The news consultants said you didn't, that good news – or miracles – wouldn't "sell," not to mention that a reporter who admitted to seeing miracles would probably find her next career move to some "bureau" in Montana. So I sat on my secret until, well, until I got out of news and got the balls (so to speak) to share it with the world. So ...

I see miracles. There. I said it.

And no, this isn't about seeing the Virgin Mary on a grilled cheese sandwich. Although that would be pretty cool. And it's not like that kid in the movie *The Sixth Sense*, who says, "I see dead people." It's not like that. I don't have any special powers, and I don't hear voices; I don't even go to church. In fact, my life has been just as screwed up as the next person's (maybe more so in some ways, being a TV news reporter). That's why I think it's important to tell people that someone like me, someone like you, *can* see and experience miracles.

Now, I know miracles mean different things to different people. In Sunday school, Pastor Thorson taught us that miracles were when Jesus walked on water and when God wrote the Ten Commandments on stone tablets for Moses. Oh, yeah. Those definitely would be miracles. But I've come to believe that those aren't the only *kinds* of miracles. Miracles don't have to be "in your face." In fact, I believe, few of them are.

It'd be like saying that celebrities or politicians are the only "important" people. No, there are lots of us who are talented and special and contribute in our own small, anonymous ways. Call me vain, but I think it's these people, people like us, who *really* make a difference: sharing a smile, offering a hand, being good parents and friends. Small acts, maybe. Noticed? Rarely. But they can change someone's day, someone's life, for the better.

It's the same way with miracles; the small, quiet ones swirling around each of us every day, working their magic whether or not anyone notices. Simple messages from above or from God or from whatever you believe is "out there" managing all this craziness. Messages that say "Hey! You're special. Hey! You're loved. Even when you've screwed up, you're never alone, disowned, or abandoned. *I* or *we* or *it* is/are always here. Just look; just listen.

These are the kinds of miracles I see. I'm not perfect at it. I too get all caught up in my job and family and groceries and road rage and on and on. But with practice, I can get quiet and look and listen and pay attention ... and *boom!* There they are. My miracles. Just for me. To remind me that there's something bigger, better, and ultimately loving out there, something that's watching over me, always, with love.

Now I realize that I probably sound like a nut or some ethereal Goody Two-Shoes. So let me "humanize" myself a bit so you know you're not talking to someone who's going to preach at you and then hit you up for money or ask you to come live in my compound. Really. I'm just a *normal* nut.

I grew up in Chippewa Falls, Wisconsin: population 12,925 for the last forty years or so. I guess people just keep dying and giving birth at about the same rate every year. Anyway, it's one of those towns where kids can still walk to school and ride their bikes after dark, and all the ladies at the beauty shop know your business. I lived in a house on top of the "West Hill" (as opposed to the East Hill, the North Side, and the South Side. The north and south were hills too, but we never called them hills). My normal Midwestern family was comprised of a Marine Corps veteran father who fought in WWII and Korea but never talked about it and a stay-at-home mom who went and got her first job when her youngest, me, went into first grade. I had two much-older brothers: Mike, seventeen years older, who went into the Marine Corps like my dad, and Steve, seven years older, who tended to get into things that would piss off my dad—and then *he* joined the Marines. Then there I was, the youngest and the only girl. To this day, my brothers remind me that I was spoiled. My mom said that too. Actually, I think that by the time I came along, my parents were just too tired of child-rearing to put any effort into denying me much.

Lest you think, though, that I had a princess upbringing that led me to this miracle business, let me explain. My dad was an alcoholic—part of his legacy from the war. And we, his family, were the Enablers. Kind of like the Cleavers, but with a dirty family secret. Even when Mom kicked Dad out after several attempts at sobering him up, I was ordered to tell neighbors and anyone else who asked that Dad was simply "on a trip"—*for a year and a half.* It was during that year and a half that I finally figured out that Dads weren't supposed to fall asleep in their La-Z-Boy recliners every night by eight with drinks in their hands. And that most kids weren't treated like boot-camp recruits who'd get in big trouble if "The Colonel" couldn't bounce a quarter off of their freshly made beds.

Fast forward through grade school and high school. I was the perfect student but had no confidence, constantly worrying that I'd screw up somehow or disappoint my parents. I didn't get into drinking, drugs, or partying. I guess that's one good side effect of seeing my dad drinking. I didn't even *want* to go there. But, when I went to college, I did do the eating-disorder thing—anorexia. It was a control issue, they tell me. To this day, I can't see my body normally. In my head, I'm still fat. I rely on my husband and good girlfriends to give me reality checks, so I don't go back to eating one hard-boiled egg and three raisins a day.

Speaking of husbands, I'm on my second one. Yup. Messed *that* up the first time! I married my college sweetheart; although, looking back, he really wasn't that sweet and didn't share much of his heart. In fact, back then he was about as deep as a puddle. It was just that we looked good together (cheerleader and star football player), and everyone expected us to get married after college. And I was such a people-pleaser by that point, I didn't even question it. Out loud, anyway. Well, I married him and found myself propelled along in a life that was definitely *not* me. He wanted the pretty, stay-at-home-mom-wife-domestic-goddess. I wanted to pursue my dream of being a television news reporter, put off having kids, and eat out. It seems to me we should have had that conversation before we got married. Then again, he and I never really talked much. So I guess that's how that happened.

When I told my parents I'd asked my husband for a divorce, my mother was so upset with me, she had only three things to say: 1) Who is going to take care of you?, 2) How will you have babies?, and 3) Who is going to want you now? After all, you're almost *thirty*. Needless to say, I went through the divorce pretty much on my own and lived paycheck to paycheck, because even when I got the divorce settlement, I was too proud to use my ex's money for anything except a savings account. I would "show" him. (Yeah, by eating Ramen noodles for a year and a half!)

So I went through my crazy, post-divorce dating and partying phase—staying out late, going to clubs, and dating a variety of guys from doctors to jocks to a twenty-something trophy boyfriend. Nothing with a future. I didn't want one. It was like I was catching up on all the fun I didn't have because I'd been with my football-player boyfriend all through college and afterward. I did have fun, I have to admit. And I did find out I could make it alone, successfully. But thank God I got out of Chicago before I burned myself out. After all, by then I *was* thirty.

That was when I got *the* TV news reporting job I'd always wanted and made the move to the Twin Cities, the market I'd always dreamed of working in. I've still had my bumps along the way with bouts of depression (which I found out, thankfully, were inherited and chemical and not simply me going crazy, so now I'm on medication and feeling much better, thank you!). And I had several more stupid relationships. Moved in with a guy, who to this day I believe was gay. He just didn't know it. Then there was my final attempt at a clone of my first husband (I still had some unresolved issues, I guess), but he was more interested in spending his time with his buddies—skiing, golfing, or drinking—than with me. And for some reason, I let that be okay! What the hell … Anyway, when I broke up with him, he turned into a stalker, and I had to change my phone number and locks and even have Security at work tell him to leave me alone. Creepy.

But I see it this way. I can look back on my life and mourn all the mistakes, all the "wasted" time, or I can see the journey as an essential one—one without which I would not be who or where I am today, which is extremely happy and in a good place. I choose the latter. If it would take all that to get here, I'd do it all over again. Okay. Almost all of it. Except for the gay guy and the stalker.

So, when did I start seeing miracles? Well, I believe I've always seen them, experienced them. I just never knew what to call them. For example …

Say you're stewing about something. Maybe your relationship isn't working out. Maybe the career you went to college for has turned out to be something you hate. Or maybe you and your friend had a stupid falling-out, and you don't know what to do. In any case, you're turning it over and over in your mind, driving yourself nuts.

So you're in your car, "driving" yourself nuts. You turn on the radio, and suddenly the song that's playing speaks directly to your problem. Bad boyfriend? Maybe you'll hear that popular song by Cee Lo, "Forget You." Hmmm. Stuck in your job? "Ch-Ch-Ch-Changes …" by David Bowie. For me, well, I've been stewing over writing this book for, oh, about two hundred years, wondering how, and if, I would ever get started. Then during one of my tormented drives in to work, I turned on the radio, and Garth Brooks was singing a song called "The River," which is all about setting a course toward your dreams. Of course, I happened to tune it in right when he was singing about how you'll never realize your dreams if you don't try. As comedian Bill Engvall would say, "There's your sign!"

Anyway, the song is just what you need, and you're wondering how the hell *that* song just *happened* to be playing exactly when you needed to hear it. Well, in my opinion, hell had nothing to do with it. It was a miracle. *Your* miracle—that little piece of advice or encouragement that arrived just when you needed it.

Ever had a certain number that keeps popping up in your life? You know, the kind that, whenever you seem to look at the clock, there it is? Mine is 11:11. Now I know I'm not the only person this happens to. Even the guy who was my stalker had a special number and would remark about how it kept showing up. (I never thought I'd have something in common with a stalker.) Anyway, it pops up here and there, often at times when you're feeling overwhelmed or rushed or alone or isolated. You're all caught up in your life, and you look at a clock or a timer or a lottery ticket, and there it is: 11-11, or 7 or 13. (I believe 13 can be lucky for some people. Why not?) How about next time, instead of writing it off as coincidence, think of it as a "hello" from the universe. It's checking in and letting you know that you "count," that you're thought of, and that whatever is such a big deal at the moment pales in comparison to your importance, just as you are, in the universe. It's your personalized numerical miracle—from God or Spirit or Buddha or angels or whatever you call it—giving you a visual hello to make you stop, take a breath, and smile.

I don't blame you if you're not convinced yet. How can miracles be happening when the world seems to be going to hell in a hand basket? The economy sucks. Many people still don't have jobs. We're in a war with no end in sight. I could go on all day about what's wrong; I'm a former television news reporter, after all. But see, I think *that's* what's wrong with all of us. We focus on what's wrong—the bad and the negative—stewing and worrying over it and growing morose and overwhelmed. It's all sucking us down into this big, black, swirling vortex of hopelessness. I think the only answer to a big, black, swirling vortex is a little "sunshine reality check" from someone who has no unique standing in this world, other than the fact that I still believe there's good out there. And the way to get to where *I* am is to learn to see miracles in the dark.

So, I'm going to tell you a few stories and share a few insights from friends I've met along the way. Even if you don't believe me, at least you'll be amused. And if I can amuse you, even for a moment amidst your harried life, I'll consider it another miracle.

Chapter One: News Miracles

If It Bleeds, It Leads.

Imagine if *that* was your corporate mission statement. It was mine. It'd pretty much have to be a hot day in Minnesota (our version of a cold day in hell) before some "good" news would actually make it into the first block of the newscast. In fact, I remember one news director who, on his first day, mandated that from that day forward there would be *no more* "dancing bear"-type stories in his newscasts. Instead, he wanted viewers to run for their lives! And we'd tell them why at 10:00.

So, I guess this book is my way of getting back at those gloom-and-doom news consultants and balancing out the bad karma I sent out into the world on a daily basis. What you're about to read is the flip side of many of the bad news stories I've reported over the years, the good stuff that went on behind the scenes, even in the most horrific of circumstances. I've also included some of my own come-to-Jesus moments during my career. when a miracle or two pulled me back from the brink of cynicism.

Keep these stories in mind when you watch the news. Miracles are happening all the time, everywhere. They just rarely make it past the editor.

"Mission of the Heart"

This was the title of the hardest story I've ever had to do. Our assignment was to follow a team of heart surgeons and nurses from the Mayo Clinic on a mission to South America. They had given up their vacation time and volunteered to go there, free of charge, to perform heart surgeries for needy children. It was supposed to be a happily-ever-after story, starring a little Colombian boy named Oscar.

Oscar had been chosen by the hospital higher-ups as the best candidate for us to follow through the "mission." He had a hole in his heart—a common birth defect routinely repaired in babies in the United States. But in Colombia, such heart surgeries are a luxury. Kids there, born with holes in their hearts, are lucky to grow up at all.

This was Oscar's only chance.

We met him and his mother in the hospital conference room, and immediately I could see why they had chosen him. He was adorable, with big, big, big doe-like eyes staring out at us from behind his mother's legs and a ready smile that took over his whole face. They told us he was six years old, but he looked no more than four; his malfunctioning heart had stunted his growth that much. It also made his head and belly look too big for his body, like the kids in those "Feed the Children" commercials—another reason he was so compelling. But health-wise, he had the best prognosis. With the operation by the American doctors, he would likely live happily ever after. And we would have our story.

But telling it would be far from easy, physically or emotionally. It was so hot that when you breathed in, it felt like when you get too close to a bonfire and your nose, throat, and lungs feel like they're singed. The asphalt squished under our feet, and tar stuck to the soles of our shoes. And it wasn't as if we could simply grab a drink of water whenever we wanted. It had to be bottled water, or we would get sick. Just try to find lots of bottled water in a poverty-stricken area. Yeah, right after I turn on the air conditioning.

The poverty we saw was staggering. Haggard, scrawny men, pulling what should have been mule-drawn carts down the busy city streets. Boarded-up businesses, tiny houses with their windows busted out, and families strewn across the front stoops, trying to stay cool. And every morning at the hospital, hundreds of sick and destitute people would lean against the cast iron gates, hoping to get in and be seen—by anyone. The lucky few who did get in lay on carts or right on the floor, head to toe, one after another, in the hallways. I can close my eyes and still smell the heat and the bodies and the faint attempts at disinfecting the place while trying to accommodate so many patients.

Our one bright spot was little Oscar. The day before surgery, we caught up with him as he skipped along beside his mother on their way into the hospital. He was dressed in his best plaid, short-sleeved shirt and pants, like a tiny man. His wee hand wrapped around his mother's fingers. He was so happy and not at all intimidated by this big building or all the strange people in white coats—or us. He squirmed impishly on his mother's lap as she got him registered. Then we watched the two of them walk down the long, dim hallway—the silhouette of mother and child—to the room where Oscar would spend the night before his big day. To celebrate, his mother had bought him new pajamas, which he demanded to put on right away, even though it was early afternoon.

His "room" was far from private. At least a dozen other sick children lay on crib-like carts, wedged in wall-to-wall in the stark, tiled room. Most of them had no visitors. Most of them seemed used to that. I remember this one girl in particular, a teenager, her thick, black hair in clumpy braids on top of her head, her body merely a wrinkle in the sheet that covered it. But she had the biggest smile as she watched us—as if she was grateful for the diversion. She smiled even bigger when we took her picture. It was such a small thing—to us, anyway.

Oscar wasn't the first child the surgical teams operated on the next morning. When we were escorted into the pre-op area, they were already hard at work on another little boy's heart. And there was Oscar, sitting all alone on the edge of a cart in the hallway outside the OR. He didn't try to get down or run away. In fact, the only sign of his impatience was one big sigh his little chest heaved as yet another nurse passed him by without any acknowledgment.

Then Oscar saw us—someone he knew!—and his whole head smiled. We began videotaping as one of the American nurses he'd met in the big conference room came to get him. He wriggled with delight. "Oscar!" she said. "Hola, little peanut!" I could see his eyes shining up at her. We followed him into the operating room where all of the doctors and nurses openly adored him. I don't think he'd ever had so much attention. I remember the line I wrote about that moment when Oscar "stole the hearts of the doctors who would be fixing his." We got a close-up of Oscar covering his face like in peek-a-boo as he giggled. Then the mask went over his mouth, and he was asleep.

The surgery went well—a textbook case, just like they'd hoped. The same wasn't true for that first little boy who'd had the operation before Oscar's. As the American surgeon finished with Oscar, he responded to an urgent call from the recovery room, where the first little boy was struggling to breathe. With Oscar in good hands, we raced along behind the surgeon to film what was happening. It turned out that one of the little boy's lungs had collapsed, which sometimes happens after heart surgery, and is entirely treatable. With the help of an interpreter, the doctor and nurses calmed his hysterical mother. And as the boy's breathing eased up in response to their efforts, we all breathed a little easier. He was going to be fine.

Just like Oscar. We turned the camera around just as Oscar was being wheeled down the hallway to recover next to the first little boy. Nurses told his mother how well he'd done, and she cried as she stroked his forehead. We watched and recorded as she took her place among the tangle of tubes that continued to help Oscar breathe and gave his newly repaired heart a little help. The last thing I remember seeing was the mother's head nestled on his shoulder and her hand holding his, just as it had when they'd walked into the hospital the day before.

We went back to our hotel, grateful that the hardest and longest part of our shoot was over. Once you're in the operating room, you're pretty much stuck there for the duration; they don't want you to contaminate anything by going in and out. So that meant that the photographer and I had been on our feet for more than twelve hours. Food, bed, and then a short day comprised of our happily-ever-after moment: that's what we were planning.

But Oscar had a different plan.

Overnight, we heard the surgeons get paged out to the hospital. We rushed over soon after, assuming that the first little boy was in trouble again. But no, this time it was Oscar. At least five times during the night, the little guy's heart had stopped beating. And the moment we arrived, it stopped again.

In a flurry of hands and words and needles and paddles, the entire surgical team worked to bring Oscar back. The tape they use to keep patients' eyelids shut as they recover from anesthesia had come loose, letting the lids lift far enough to show Oscar's big doe-eyes rolled back into his head. He wasn't responding. The next thing we knew, the surgeon's hands were inside Oscar's chest, having cut back through the incisions, pumping his little heart for him. "Come on, little guy, come on" we heard him say. His surgical mask sucked in and out in desperation. Above it, I could see that his eyes were wet. The photographer and I couldn't believe what was happening. Oscar seemed to be dying right before our eyes. We looked on, bewildered, as the surgeon finally pulled his hands out of Oscar's chest and told the nurses to go get his mother. Then he turned to us. "His heart just never recovered from the stress of the surgery. The hole in it had gone untreated too long. He was simply too weak, too weak."

He turned to Oscar's mother to explain as best as he could what had happened. The interpreter stroked her arm as she translated, then Oscar's mother fell into the arms of the American nurses, sobbing.

Dumbfounded. Devastated. That's the only way I can explain that moment. It's like we all stood there, waiting for Oscar to wake up and give us our "happily ever after." Instead, he lay motionless with his mother sobbing at his side. Between sobs she thanked everyone for trying to save her son, for giving him his chance at life.

But what about the "mission?"—hers, the surgical team's, ours? This story was supposed to be about *saving* lives. Saving Oscar's life. But our poster child for success had died.

After Oscar's tiny body had been wheeled out and the tears cried out, my photographer and I went to sit outside on the hospital steps. It seemed cruel that it was so bright and sunny right then. We didn't say anything, but our minds were racing. We were supposed to go home the next day with our "success story." Then the head surgeon came up and asked us what everybody had been wondering.

"What are you going to do now? There's no time to profile another kid."

I looked up at him. "I'm going to say that he died."

The surgeon and the PR-types who had orchestrated the whole thing were flabbergasted. How could I report on a child who had died, when their message was all about saving lives? Who would support their mission without seeing the happily-ever-after it was supposed to accomplish?

But that's where we all were wrong. The story about Oscar's death, despite the best efforts of the best surgeons in the world, was more powerful than any "success story." It was picked up by stations throughout the country. People who saw it cried, mortified that lives so easy to save were simply a casualty of poverty. Oscar made them want to help. Oscar motivated them to act.

The organization that facilitated the mission, Children's Heartlink, got calls and donations from all over the country. More missions were organized. More doctors went down. More lives *were* saved because of Oscar's death.

Looking back, I realize that our real "mission" was to tell his story. We were destined to meet him, destined to fall in love with him, destined to feel—and communicate—his tragic loss. To make people aware. To make a difference. That's what Oscar's miracle was—his "Mission of the Heart."

"Get the Mother"

My heart sank. It was the assignment all reporters dread. "Go talk to the mother of the shooting victim," our assignment editor said. "Here's the address."

It hadn't been but a few hours since the boy had died, his family's one shining star. He was the one who was going to "make it"—make it out of poverty, out of the 'hood,' even make it into college. He had gotten good grades in school and offers from college basketball teams. He was seventeen. And now he was dead.

He was the atypical victim of a typical drive-by shooting in one of Minneapolis's more dangerous neighborhoods. The shooting was a gang thing, not meant for him. But he was at the wrong place at the wrong time. And as I approached his family's home—the old but fiercely kept-up one with all the shades pulled down—I cursed my job. I expected to be yelled at or to have the door slammed in my face at the least. It would serve me right.

Slowly I walked up the cement steps, the iron railing wobbling in my grip. I knocked three times, breathed in deeply once, and held it. A younger teenage boy came to the door. The kid brother, I thought. Damn! Now what's going to happen to him, seeing how his brother died?

"Hi, I'm Kris Patrow from Channel 5. Is there anyone at home who can tell me about your brother?"

The boy's eyes went darker, turned downward, and he mumbled, "Just a minute." He partially closed the door as he turned to walked back inside, as if light itself wasn't welcome there.

My heart pounded. The door hadn't slammed. But I had freshened the boy's pain. I could feel it.

Then a bigger hand, a woman's hand, gripped the door and pulled it wide. Her swollen eyelids were barely able to blink back the sunlight. Though I'd never seen her before, I knew right away who she was: the mother.

"Ma'am, I am *so* sorry about your son and so sorry to be bothering—"

That was it. That was enough. I saw her eyes widen with anger as she sidled her body between me and what was left of her family.

"How dare you! How *dare* you come here...," and off she went, voicing every terrible thing I expected her to yell at me, everything she was justified in saying. She was right. How dare I? I stood there, heart pounding and wincing at every word. My photographer stood helplessly behind me on the step, ready to book at my signal. But I gave none. It was the least I could do after being such an ass. I should at least let her yell at me. I bowed my head.

After a few eternal minutes, her voice hoarse with sobs faded; but she didn't slam the door. She just stood there, all the grief and anger and helplessness in the world trapped in one body. Her heavy shoulders heaved with the sobs that had run out. I dared to look up. I dared to ask ...

"What do you want people to know about your son? What do you want me to tell them?"

She could have told me to go to hell. She could have told me worse than that. But, she cocked her head like no one had asked her that before. And in her eyes rose a new determination. She said nothing, but she disappeared back into the house and re-emerged with photo albums and scrapbooks spilling over with newspaper articles and awards.

The screen door creaked as she opened it. "This ... this is my boy," she said. She nodded at the photographer, who hoisted his camera onto his shoulder and rolled. "What I want people to know about my boy is that he was a fine young man. You see here? This is when he got all A's in grade school; he even won the spelling bee that year. And here? Here's where he got to play on the all-varsity basketball team when he was just a freshman. Scored six points that night. Oh—and this is when he volunteered for ..."

It was as if I had uncorked a bottle that held a wonderful genie inside. Here were all the stories and accomplishments and hopes that this boy had made in his short life—the ones that would keep him alive for his mama, for everyone. And now, through me, they would be kept alive even for those who hadn't known him.

It was then that I realized something. Perhaps at this most terrible time, this poor mother first needed someone to yell at and get out all of her anger at the world; and second, she needed someone to tell that same world what it would be missing now and what it should remember about her boy. I believe I was sent to be her miracle that day.

"Seeing the Light"

It was the kind of day every news crew dreads yet is bound to experience. My photographer Dave and I had gotten our assignment late: a little girl dying of heart failure at the Mayo Clinic. Her family was pleading for help. It was an important story, the kind that Dave and I could do very well. But we were getting a late start, and Rochester was an hour and a half away.

So we had that going against us. In addition to that stress, we each had our personal dramas to contend with—his divorce, my neglectful boyfriend. So we spent a good portion of our hour-and-a-half drive just venting.

The story itself went very well. We met up with the girl's parents outside the hospital and recorded their story about their brave little girl who at first seemed to have a mild case of the flu—until her inexplicable spiral downward as the virus attacked her heart. A transplant was her only hope, and time was running out.

We barely made our deadline, feeding it back to the station via our satellite truck and introducing it live from Rochester. But there it was: we'd gotten the word out about organ donation and how this little girl's life hung in the balance. Dave and I were so proud, until ...

Until the news anchor back at the station asked me a totally stupid question, live, on the air. Stupid because the answer to his question had been thoroughly covered in the story (i.e., he hadn't paid attention). I was so flabbergasted that I stumbled in my answer, making myself look just as stupid. After all that work.

Well, poor Dave. I got in the news car for the long drive home and began ranting and raving about our stupid anchor, and how dare he ask such a dumb question, and now how would the story fare, and I looked so stupid, and on and on. I didn't even come up for air until I happened to glance out my passenger side window.

"Dave, pull over!"

"Why?"

"Just pull over!"

He signaled off onto a dirt road and parked. And there, as we got out, was the most brilliant northern lights display I had ever seen:

dancing greens and reds and yellows, undulating across the night sky. It was so awesome that neither of us dared to breathe, let alone speak. The display went on for what seemed like forever—forever, until waves of light above us were matched by waves of calm within. I turned to Dave.

"Everything is going to be okay."

"What do you mean?"

"Everything. That little girl. Your divorce. My bad boyfriend. It's all going to be okay. I just know."

When we got back to the station, we asked the satellite-truck driver what he thought of the northern lights. (He had been driving right behind us.) He said, "What northern lights?" And in fact, nobody else we talked to had seen them that night. I started to wonder if they were a message meant just for us.

A week or so later, that little girl got her heart transplant and made a miraculous recovery. Dave survived his divorce, and my bad relationship got better because, well, I ended it. That night taught me that life is too precious to be wasted on things (or people) that either won't change or don't really matter in the first place.

"Prisoner of War"

Dave couldn't have been more excited about the story he was about to do. It was his first job out of college, and the station he worked for, WHO-TV in Des Moines, had started a new series called "Through the Lens" in which photojournalists could showcase their own stories. Being young and new and wanting to show off his skills, like all young journalists do, Dave jumped at the opportunity. With the fiftieth anniversary of the Battle of Iwo Jima coming up, he had found a local veteran and Iwo Jima survivor to interview. He knew that with a few compelling sound bites, shots of some war memorabilia, and some historical footage, he could create a very moving story.

It was February of 1995. Dave remembers that it was a bright, sunny summer day. Bob, the old Marine he'd set up the interview with, opened the door wearing a crisp, white shirt and khaki pants: very neat and clean—Bob and his apartment. He introduced Dave to his granddaughter, who he assumed was there to make sure he treated her grandfather right. Dave noticed that there was no wife, only pictures of her. Bob was in his seventies, so he was probably a widower.

Bob couldn't have been nicer as Dave painstakingly set up his lights and his camera in the living room. They talked comfortably from the get-go, with him addressing Bob as "sir" (out of respect for his age and what he'd done for our country), and Bob treating him like some long-lost grandson. This made Dave even *more* excited about his story, since the more open the old veteran was, the better the story would turn out.

Bob sat down. Looking back, Dave says his lighting was way too harsh: blinding and interrogation-like—a common new-photojournalist mistake. But Bob didn't complain.

Dave turned the camera on. But instead of standing behind it like most photojournalists do, Dave says he somehow knew he should just lock it down in place and walk away, let the old man forget he was being interviewed. Dave sat down to the side and asked simply, "What was it like?"

Well, it was as if the old Marine had been waiting to tell his story all these fifty years. Immediately he was back on the beaches of Iwo Jima, he and his brother sitting midway back on a landing craft sardined with the other soldiers, cresting the waves on the way to shore. Upon command, the front of the landing craft dropped down, and instantly all the men in front of Bob and his brother were shot and killed by enemy fire. A huge wave mercifully threw Bob and his brother over the side as the bullets whirred by. They used their fellow-soldiers' dead bodies as shields as they made their way onto the beach. From body to body, toward the enemy. For what seemed like an eternity.

Dave says that if the old man hadn't been sitting there telling him these things to his face, he wouldn't have believed it. It was like something a movie producer would dream up to make a scene more horrific. Only here it was, in this man's memory, making his eyes water and his hands tremble and his voice speak haltingly as he choked back the tears. For Bob, it was as real as the day it had happened. He kept saying how those men who died in front of him, their bodies protecting him, were the real heroes of Iwo Jima. Not him. Not him.

That one question was pretty much all Dave asked the old man. His story spent, Bob got up and left the room to collect himself. It was then that his granddaughter came up to Dave and thanked him for being so nice to her grandfather. She said that although he had spoken of the war, she had never heard all these tragic details of his experience, that he must have been holding them inside all these years. A prisoner of the war.

Dave knew then that this story was not so much about him or a vehicle for showing off his talents. More than that, *he was a vehicle* meant to give this old man a way to release his memories, to tell people what he wanted them to know about that horrific battle and his buddies. It was a way for the old soldier to heal.

Dave put the story together just as the old man told it: simply, with some historic footage of the battle edited in to help illustrate the man's memories. Yes, the story did get the kudos Dave had originally set out to get. But the real reward, the miracle of it all, was in how that one story changed Dave's mind forever about his role as a journalist, how his job wasn't about showing off, winning awards, and impressing his colleagues. It was about helping people tell their stories, getting their messages out to the people who needed to hear them—in the most responsible, sensitive way he could.

That the old veteran had lived to tell his story about Iwo Jima was a miracle in itself. That he in turn was able to share his experience with thousands of others, just when *he* needed to most, was another. That he changed the course of one young journalist's life and the hundreds of stories he would go on to tell is the miracle that Dave's been blessed with ever since.

"Cold Hands, Warm Heart"

I was looking for mittens and found a miracle.

It was, as usual, a bitterly cold Minnesota day; so of course I got assigned a story that took place outside and required that I "go live" outside for the five- and six-o'clock news. Lucky me.

It *was* lucky that I was working with one of the station's best photographers, who went by the nickname of "Werthy" (short for Wertheimer). In addition to being a good friend and very talented at his job, Werthy knew all the tricks for surviving any kind of weather. Most of them were packed in this news van. We used to joke that should Armageddon come, we'd all pile in Werthy's van and be able to live quite well for weeks while he went out and videotaped Armageddon. And if, perchance, Werthy *didn't* have a particular weather-survival item, he knew where to get it.

That's why we stopped at this obscure, outdoor-outfitters store on our way to our story. I needed some mittens or gloves that actually made sense (not those skin-thin Isotoners that look great but allow your fingers to freeze into icicles in thirty-below weather); and this was a place where Werthy had shopped before. While he went off to find the latest arctic photographers' gear, I pawed through a bin of sheepskin mittens and found a pair of red ones that didn't match anything but were sure to keep my hands from falling off. Plus, red is my favorite color, so I decided to buy them.

I met Werthy up at the counter, and as I was waiting to pay, a small display of CDs next to the cash register caught my eye. They were entitled *Opus Derian* and had a sweet picture of a little boy on the front. The sign next to it said that they were being sold to raise money for a local charity.

As a reporter, you learn to pay attention to things like this. Wherever there's a charity, there's usually a compelling story about how and why it got started. So I asked the store manager about it, and he told me that Derian was the son of a friend of his, that Derian had died, and that in his memory, his parents had created a charity to help other families with sick kids. The store manager gave me the dad's name and phone number on the back of his business card. I bought a CD, tucked it in my work bag, put on my new mittens, and forgot about it till the next day.

The father's name was Robert Keech; when I called, it was his wife Patsy who answered. She had such a bright, hopeful, and childlike voice, it was hard to believe that the woman it belonged to had suffered such a terrible loss. When I sheepishly told her why I was calling (I had the vulture-reporter guilt going again), she sounded like she was going to jump through the phone—not to beat me, but to hug me. Of course she'd love for me to do a story! Oh, it would help the charity so much! And she would love people to know about her precious son Derian.

Dave Ogle (my future husband) and I got to do the story. I remember it was sometime between Thanksgiving and Christmas, and as we drove to South St. Paul where the Keeches lived, we talked about the most sensitive way to handle this story: what elements we should make sure to get, how to respect their grief.

I remember driving up to their house, a cozy, one-story, longish house. A medium-sized kitchen window on the left, then the front door, then a couple of smaller windows to the right. The garage was set back and away from the house at the end of a long, snowplowed driveway. It was dark outside (so it must have been after 4:00 p.m.), but every window glowed with warm, yellowish light. And I could see Christmas decorations inside.

Patsy greeted us with twinkly eyes and a huge smile. Her cheeks were round, sitting on top of what seemed to be a perpetual smile; she looked to be in her early thirties. Only her eyes looked somewhat older after what she had gone through. Her husband Rob was a little more subdued, a big guy with a soft but ready grin, and their other son Kevin was just as welcoming and open as his mom.

Instead of a house that was mourning someone's death and trying to put it behind them, I found that the Keeches' home was festive and that it celebrated Derian's life. His pictures were everywhere, just like Kevin's—family photos and art projects. His ornaments were on the Christmas tree. I finally realized that I did not have to grieve for this family, that the greatest respect I could show would be to ask all about their beloved Derian and to help others to celebrate him too.

We sat Patsy and Rob down on the floor in front of their Christmas tree. They told us how Derian had been born with a rare congenital disease, how he had had multiple surgeries and near-death struggles throughout his short two-and-a-half-year life. Patsy and Rob had spent most of their time—and money—at the hospital. It was only by the generosity of others that they had been able to pay their bills and keep their house.

So when Derian died, Patsy was motivated to do something to pay them back. Derian had brought out so much love and generosity in people, she decided the best way to honor his life was to do the same for others. So she established the Spare Key Foundation, to help pay the mortgages for families with sick kids, so they didn't have to worry about missing work to be at the hospital with their children. With simple fundraisers like 5K runs, bake sales, and even that CD I'd found, the money came pouring in—as if it was all meant to be. Patsy said it was Derian's miracle—at least one of them, anyway. "By the way, how did that CD come about?" we asked. She smiled and immediately got on the phone. When she hung up, she said that the CD's composer, Steven C. Anderson, would answer that question if we could get to his house within the hour. Dave shot the necessary photos of Derian; then we thanked them profusely and raced north to St. Paul.

Steven C. Anderson lived in a beautiful Victorian mansion on St. Paul's storied Summit Avenue, not far from the governor's mansion. Approaching his house, I kind of expected to meet some hoity-toity musician guy wearing an ascot and smoking expensive cigars. But then Steven C. opened the door—in blue jeans and a nondescript sweater, with a mop of blond hair falling over a very kind and humble forty-something face. He had a baby grand right there in his living room, where he took his place on the bench like he would on a sofa. We mic'd him up, and he began to tell us his Derian story.

Steven C. had been asked by the pastor of an area church to play at an event. He had agreed to meet with the pastor and see what kind of organ they had in the church. It was early evening, and when Steven walked into the church, it was empty—empty save for a small coffin draped in white up at the altar. He told us how he was drawn to it, despite his being a father himself and aching at the thought of how devastated this child's parents must be. But he couldn't help it. And as he approached the tiny casket, a melody filled his mind, so familiar he thought he must have heard it somewhere before. But it built, one note upon the other, and the closer he got, the more he knew he was supposed to sit down and play it, to write it down.

It was then that the pastor came in and told Steven C. about the tiny boy who lay there. He apologized that he hadn't greeted Steven at the door and guided him to the correct room for their meeting. But Steven somehow knew he was meant to be there, to see Derian's casket. As soon as he got home, he sat down and played the melody and wrote it all down. He contacted Patsy out of the blue and told her what he'd done and asked what he should do with it now. And that's how the CD for the fundraiser was born: Derian Miracle Number Two.

Our hearts were so full and humbled by these generous, selfless people, and by the miracle of how this all came together, that our story pretty much wrote itself. We let Patsy and Rob and Steven do the talking; we let Steven's music set the mood and the charity make its voice heard. Many of us teared up watching it, and I remember Patsy calling me as soon as it had aired, with joyful gratitude in her voice.

And Derian hasn't stopped there. Since our story back in 1998, The Spare Key Foundation has helped more than one thousand families make ends meet while their children have been in the hospital. Patsy has appeared on the Oprah Winfrey show and has been honored by then Minnesota Governor Tim Pawlenty for her efforts on behalf of Minnesota families in need. At the time of this writing, Derian's legacy has brought in more than $1 million dollars. His miracle lives on.

"Nursing a Hunch"

The assignment editor paged Dave and me to the desk. "That nursing home in Rochester is closing—something about neglecting patients. Go down there and see if somebody will talk."

This, in assignment-desk language, means, *No one's talking. Go and annoy someone until they yell at you.*

Dave and I were working on the ten o'clock news that night. We'd gotten the assignment late, so, without a single phone call, we jumped into the news van and headed the hour and a half south to Rochester. On the way, I called everyone I knew down there (I used to work at the NBC station in town). No one had any contacts—at least none who would talk. In Rochester, home of the Mayo Clinic, anything resembling inadequate patient care is so unthinkable that no one can even fathom it, much less acknowledge it happening. So this bad nursing home had become the town's dirty, little secret.

About twenty minutes outside of town, it began pouring rain, the summer kind of rain that hits hot pavement and then rises up as steam in front of you. So now it was going to be a bad-hair day on top of a bad-news-story day, I thought. Dave asked me what we should do. I answered honestly that I didn't know, that he should just drive around town until I thought of something.

Sometimes when you're assigned an impossible news story, you can drive around and maybe see a storefront sign or newspaper headline or directions to a county fair that triggers an idea for telling it. Not this time. It was night; it was raining; and it was conservative Rochester. That's why Dave about wrecked the car when I suddenly demanded that he pull over next to an old coffee shop.

What? Why? He heaved, looking in the side-view mirror to see if the Rochester police were going to make him step out for a sobriety test.

"I don't know," I said. "I just have this feeling that we're supposed to go in there."

It was the old coffee shop across from the Mayo Clinic where a lot of patients and their families wait for their appointments and subsequently their news. I had gone there back in 1992 with my mom and brothers when my dad had surgery for throat cancer. I remembered it being appropriately cheerful, with plastic, red-and-white-checked tablecloths decorated with fake sprays of flowers in those unashamedly fake-fancy white vases, and waitresses who still wore pastel "nurse/waitress" uniforms with white lacy aprons tied neatly behind their waists in a bow. I half expected them to still have beehive hairdos, but most of them had progressed to either Farrah-hair or Mall-bangs or both.

I still had no idea why I felt drawn there, so I simply went up to the hostess stand and said, "Hi, I'm Kris Patrow. I'm a reporter with Channel 5 in the Twin Cities. We're doing a story on that nursing home outside of town that's being closed down. I was wondering if it would be okay for us to go around and ask any of your customers if they know anything about it."

I thought I must sound like a crazy person or a typical news-vulture. But the lady acted like she had been expecting me. "Oh, you know, our waitress so-and-so's sister has a mother-in-law who's at that nursing home. She's really upset about the whole thing. Let me get her for you."

And that was that. Before I knew it, the waitress had hooked us up with her sister and brother-in-law to do an interview in their home, complete with pictures of the mother-in-law and their sad story about the neglect she'd suffered there. It was exactly the personal perspective we needed to tell a responsible story.

On our way back that night, Dave asked me how I knew to stop at that coffee shop. I said I just knew. My gut told me. Truth was, I knew, from many years of *not* listening to my gut, that it might behoove me once in a while to just go with it. And now I understood why. When you're faced with what seems to be humanly impossible, go beyond the humanly understandable for your answer.

"Icebreaker"

It was one of those famous Minnesota days where people were running around in their shirt-sleeves because it was all of 32 degrees outside. My assignment that day: to do a story about how it was time for people to get their ice-fishing houses off the lakes before they melted through and fell in. Now, we do this story every spring; nevertheless, some yahoo always waits a little too long and winds up risking life, limb, and pickup truck, trying to pull his half-submerged ice-fishing house out of the lake. Then that becomes the follow-up story. Very predictable, wet, and cold. So I was less than excited.

My photographer, John, though, couldn't have been happier. On the way to the lake, he talked about neat ways he could shoot the story and the cool people we might interview. When we got there, he bounded out onto the lake ahead of me, eager to find that perfect sinking ice house to film.

Let me tell you a little about John. At one time, he had been *the* sports anchor at a major station in Detroit. Famous. Big salary. Great house and family. Then suddenly he lost his job. No warning. The sudden hiatus forced him to do some soul-searching. Back before his path had led him to anchoring sports, he'd always loved being behind the camera. His young-man's dreams were of being a photojournalist. So, at age fifty, with a family to feed and a mortgage to pay, he began applying for photographer jobs. The only one he could get was a part-time gig at a small station in Indiana, but if ever he was to live his dream, that was his chance. So he drove there, lived in his car, showered at the truck stop, and sent every cent home to keep his family housed and fed. It was a long, hard journey for him, but eventually he realized his dream of working at KSTP in Minneapolis, the number-one photojournalism station in the country.

By photographer standards, John was "old." In his fifties, he was somewhat overweight, with a back and knees that weren't too happy about the sudden shift into physical labor. As I watched him huff and puff his way out onto the lake, I noticed that he was wearing loafers, not boots, with only thin socks on. And his pants were only that thin polyester material that's neither wind- nor waterproof. No hat, no gloves. Just his jacket that boasted KSTP's prestigious selection as national photography station of the year.

I sloshed my way out behind him, thinking him more crazy than optimistic. Methodically, I found people to interview and ice-fishing houses to shoot. Cynically I wondered which one was going to be the idiot who let his house (and probably his truck and himself) fall into the lake this year. John, on the other hand, was genuinely, incredibly interested in what everyone had to say. He thanked each person heartily for sharing their time and their stories. And when we'd done enough interviews, he asked whether I minded if he went and got some more cool shots for our story.

I looked at him. His feet were soaked. His thin pants lapped against his legs in the chill wind. I was anxious to get back to the car, so I said, go ahead. You could almost see the slush kick up behind him as he scampered further out onto the ice.

About halfway back to the car, I heard a yell. It was so loud it made me jump and wonder whether John had fallen through the ice. I squinted and saw John, a mere speck in the distance, kneeling down into the slush in order to film a better angle of the ice houses. He looked at me, jumped up, and yelled again, waving his arms in the air: "Hey! Isn't this great? Isn't this *just great?*"

Suddenly I saw the world through John's eyes: the sun shining so brightly that it made particle rainbows out of the blowing snow, the sky cloudless and the kind of blue that kids color it in grade school. The ice fishermen were kindly bent over their fishing poles, the picture of patience against a relentless wind.

We weren't stuck in an office on this beautiful day. Instead, we got to go out and meet nice people in the beautiful Minnesota wilderness *and* have the privilege of telling their stories. And the bonus was that perhaps our story would help prevent the kind of tragedy I cynically expected would happen.

It was *appreciation*, in the form of a fifty-something man who was just beginning to live his dream—learned by a reporter who had almost taken hers for granted.

"Lost and Found in Romania"

It was the bitterly frigid winter of 1990. I had been dispatched with a camera crew to ride along with a convoy of trucks carrying relief supplies from Leeds, England, to Iasi, Romania. Lions Clubs International had organized the mission to help the thousands of displaced orphans from the Ceausescu regime. Under his rule, couples had been mandated to have as many children as possible to fatten up the ranks of his armies; then, when the regime collapsed and parents couldn't afford to care for all of these babies, they became wards of the state. The orphanages were overcrowded, filthy, and understaffed; and everything—from the most basic medical supplies to diapers and blankets—was nearly impossible to find. This convoy of trucks was stuffed with everything the Lions could think of to make the children's lives a little more comfortable and give them a somewhat better chance at growing up.

I remember we were somewhere in Germany when we heard on the BBC that the Gulf War had broken out. The United States was mounting an unprecedented air and ground campaign to bring Saddam Hussein to his knees. Anti-American sentiment was high as we crossed into the Eastern Bloc; we were even stopped for several hours on the border between Hungary and Czechoslovakia, for no apparent reason other than that we were Americans. Armed guards marched in circles around our van, occasionally scraping away the ice from the windows to peer in, wave their rifles a little, and then continue marching.

In spite of the politics, our convoy was often greeted with cheers and chased by children as we made our way through the tiny villages. Grown-ups waved, and we began throwing handfuls of candy out to the children as we passed—that is, until we saw some parents pushing their own children down in order to get the candy. That was the first moment I realized how desperate this part of the world was.

The second time was when our convoy pulled into the town square of Iasi, Romania, our destination city. Everything—I mean *everything*— was a shade of gray: buildings, sidewalks, streets, apartment buildings; even the snow was gray. People were doing that hurried-cold walk, heads down against the wind in their thin, gray, wool coats. I noticed that most people didn't even have hats or gloves, and that the only leg-covering many of the women had against the chill was nylon stockings or thin cotton tights with holes in them.

So there we came, all decked out in our rainbow of goose-down-filled jackets, insulated pants, and shin-high boots from L.L. Bean, topped off with puffy hats and mittens that made us look like the Michelin Man. I felt embarrassed, as if we were mocking these people who had so little and who were so cold. I'd had no idea.

They stared at us with tired eyes, the way babies do when they're still too young to know that it's not polite. In my discomfort, I looked around for any friendly face. Instead, my eyes came to rest on an image that is forever burned into my heart: the bare, bony ankles of a little boy. He seemed to be about eight years old, very thin, with short, sandy-brown hair that wasn't long enough to cover his red, bare ears. He stood with his bare hands shoved down into his wool coat, shifting from foot-to-foot in his worn-out loafers and too-short pants. I looked at his eyes. He was staring too, but it was a soft kind of stare that still had a little hope in it. Then suddenly, he was gone.

The stares continued as we went about our mission of delivering the supplies to the orphanages. What started out as my feeling oh-so-generous about all the supplies we were bringing turned into a feeling of desperation for how it didn't even come close to all that was needed here.

The babies: I remember those poor, skinny babies with their big, round eyes made bigger by being malnourished, hanging on to the edges of their creaky cribs, one against another against another. Most of those babies were clothed only in makeshift cloth diapers, and they were more excited to see people than any of the things we brought with us, because there were only a few nurses to care for dozens and dozens of abandoned children.

This story is getting harder to write, the more I remember.

And every day, I remember, I seemed to catch a glimpse of that same eight-year-old boy I saw on our first day there. He'd suddenly just be there, on the periphery of whatever we were doing, shivering in his thin coat and no socks. He never came up to us, just followed us everywhere, like a thin, saucer-eyed, little shadow.

It was the day before we were supposed to leave when we found out that our flight had been cancelled. Indefinitely. Fallout from the Gulf War, we were told. We would have to stay in Iasi until a military plane could fly us to Bucharest, where we could pick up a commercial flight out of the country.

There was nothing left for us to do except wait. So we decided to walk around the city to waste a few hours and hopefully return to the hotel for good news about our departure.

We felt very lucky, then, when we came upon a busy farmer's market in the middle of town. It was the first time we had heard music and laughter all week, and the booths actually had items that contained some color and foods other than breads and cheeses.

My crew and I decided to split up because we all wanted to see different things. I was particularly drawn to a table full of beautifully woven and embroidered wraps—perhaps a gift for my mom, I thought as I squeezed my way toward the booth.

Now, like I said, it was very crowded to begin with. So when people started pushing from behind me, I didn't take much notice. But when I turned around to leave, I realized that they were pushing and grabbing at me—this cluster of older women, draped in thin shawls, their weathered faces all talking at once in Romanian—as they pinned me against the table. I can still see the flurry of hands frantically pulling at my clothes—my jacket, my gloves, my earmuffs, anything that was warmer than what they had on, which was pretty much everything. I remember their eyes, so sunken and dark … not mean, not threatening, just desperate for any piece of the warmth that I had.

Still, I was scared to death. I remember swinging my elbows around, trying to break their grasp. I could feel my heart beating hard, imagining myself being trampled and stripped before anyone could help me. After twisting and turning and pushing for what seemed like forever, I broke free. The women's arms followed me in that reaching kind of way that you see on TV when they're handing out food to the hungry. I ran and ran and ran. I didn't realize that they'd actually unzipped my jacket and taken my earmuffs off of my head and one mitten off my hand until I was a couple of blocks away.

With my heart still pounding and a couple of nervous glances behind me, I started making my way back to the hotel. And then, suddenly, there he was: the eight-year-old boy, standing right in front of me as if he had simply materialized out of the blowing snow. My first instinct was to run past him in case he too wanted to yank something off of me. Then I saw what he had in his hands: my earmuffs and my mitten. With no expression on his face, he held them out to me.

"Madam?" his small-boy voice offered.

Now, I don't know how, but this little waif of a child had somehow gotten my earmuffs and mitten back for me. Lord knows what he went through to pry them from the hands of those women. Plus, he could have kept them. He could have (God, *should* have) put those earmuffs on his bright red little ears and the cozy mitten on his pale little hand. But he had not. Again he offered, "Madam?"

I had to help him somehow. I remember our organizers telling us that people here really valued things like chocolate, cigarettes, and American blue jeans. But I had none of those. So I reached in my zipper pocket and pulled out some dollar bills. The little boy's eyes widened as they soaked in the view of my hand, like the dollars were something in a fairy tale that he couldn't believe was true. His small, cracked lips hung open, his gaze never leaving my hand as I walked up to him and "paid" him for my earmuffs and mitten. His fingers wrapped around those dollars so quick that they crinkled like a bow-tie, and in a flash, like before, he was gone.

I never saw the little boy again. Thinking back, maybe he was my guardian angel—or maybe he was just someone sent to remind me that, in the midst of all of that desperation and poverty and war, there is goodness and hope to fight for.

Tips for Surviving the News

Remember: the reason that bad news *is* "news" is that it's *outside the norm.*

Back when I was reporting, we were given a minute and thirty seconds, tops, to update viewers on something as complicated as the war in Iraq. Now it's even less. So there you are, getting one person's ninety-second snapshot of what's happened in the last twenty-four hours. Believe me, there's a lot more that goes on behind the scenes (often the good news) that we reporters don't have time to tell you about.

A good friend and mentor of mine, Joe Bailey, has written a book called *Fearproof Your Life* that talks specifically about the epidemic of fear and cynicism generated by TV news. As a psychologist specializing in addiction issues, he lends a unique perspective on how news has made a business out of using fear to addict us, making us believe that we have to stay tuned to remain informed and therefore safe. The advent of the Internet has compounded this problem, with news "as it happens" (i.e., unfiltered) being reported (but not necessarily vetted), twenty-four seven. Suddenly we find ourselves unable to look away, believing that we cannot survive without it. It's a matter of over-consumption to the point where the immersion in the drama—our scary news "high"—feels like the norm.

We can get back to a more centered, less fearful, and more joyful life if we remember that we are *consumers.* We get to *choose* what we put into our heads. Think of it this way: Food doesn't *make* us fat; cigarettes don't *make* us smoke; alcohol doesn't *make* us drink. It's whether and how we *choose* to consume them that leads to obesity, smoking, or alcoholism. It's the same way with news. We can *choose* to consume news more responsibly by moderating our intake with more objective, less emotionally charged sources. There *is* good news out there. You just have to look for it. Check out those free community newspapers just inside the door at your grocery store. Open the mail from the local charity organizations; their newsletters often have inspiring stories about volunteer efforts (which may be attached to a request for donations, but they're still worth the read). Try your church bulletin or local cable access channel. You can even Google for inspirational stories on the Internet. Granted, it's not as easy as turning on the TV, but it gives good news a fighting chance in how you frame your view of the world!

Another thing Joe said really rang true with me, mostly because I'm a TV news fossil and have spent very little time away from it for the better part of twenty years. It's not the news, the media, or other people that create our reality. It's *how we think about* what's happening around us—the information we take in—that creates it. It's like each of us is the producer and director of our own internal TV shows, creating our reality from the inside out. As Joe says, realizing this one fact is very empowering and freeing. "Once we realize that we have the power to entertain thoughts or not entertain thoughts, and that our *thoughts* determine how we feel, suddenly we are empowered to create a less fearful world and actually see the many miracles that are happening at every moment of every day."

Remember (or at least let one of us older folks tell you) that long before we ever had media, people survived. Many of us grew up reading the newspaper or watching TV news once, maybe twice a day, and we were just as engaged in the world and probably more engaged in life than we are now. The world may be more connected than ever, but don't let the result of that be your disconnecting from a happy way of life.

One final piece of advice that I'm taking myself as I write this chapter. Go on periodic "news fasts" for a day, a week … whatever you can manage. Doing this pulls you out of the "drama" and allows you to actually notice the normal (and often good) stuff that's going on around you. Not that you should live life with your blinders on. But occasional "news sunglasses" wouldn't hurt.

Chapter Two: Parenting Miracles

Before I Became a Parent …

… at age thirty-nine, the allure of babies was a total mystery to me. My experiences with them were more conducive to birth control than procreation. Whenever I got on an airplane, inevitably I'd be stuck next to or in front of the screaming, squirmy twin of Satan. The one exception, I remember, was a cute, well-behaved baby, sitting next to me on her mother's lap. Until she coughed up the cud of a cracker onto her little palm and sweetly wiped it on my expensive suit sleeve. Yeah. Good times.

So the maternal instinct never really kicked in for me.

Neither did the "step-maternal" instinct when I fell in love with Dave—who was the father of five-year-old Ryan. The only stepmother I knew of was that wicked woman who locked Cinderella in a closet then went and talked to some creepy mirror about "who's the fairest of them all." But Dave was the real deal for me, and I convinced myself that I really wasn't the type to lock Ryan in a closet (although since then, I've come darn close). So I decided to take the leap and marry his dad. Boom! Insta-Mom!

Two years later, along came Sam, followed eighteen months later by Alex (both girls). And now I "get it." I get how parenting can be the hardest and the most wonderful thing, all at the same time; how parents *need* miracles sometimes just to make it through the day. And how many miracles our kids bring us at the very time we're considering selling them on eBay.

These are some parenting miracles from my life and the lives of my friends. They happen in common situations nearly every parent has been in: endless days of diapers and runny noses, the challenge of finding daycare, taking your kid to his first Easter egg hunt—common, that is, until, just like in the news, you look a little closer. Past the tantrums and the snot and the life being sucked out of you at 3 a.m. every morning for what seems like forever, there *are* miracles to be found. Maybe, like me, you just need help learning (or remembering) how to see them. That's what these stories are meant to do.

Maybe it's just me, but I think God actually sends us kids to remind us *how* to see miracles—the way we were able to do before we ever watched CNN.

Parenting can be a "mixed bag." Make sure to look for the miracles in yours.
My ever-curious stepson, Ryan, on an outing with his dad.

"EX-pectations: Meeting Ryan's Mom"

I never knew that angels could come disguised in snips and snails and puppy dog tails. This is the story of one who did.

Ryan was a mystery to me. A flurry of a five-year-old, chock-full of chatter. This "being," this busy boy-child of my soon-to-be beloved husband, was soon to be my stepson. And I was terrified.

Ryan wasn't. He'd openly study me from across the dinner table, or from under it, as the mood hit him. He'd surprise me with a hug, then a tantrum, then ask me to color with him, all in a matter of minutes. He wanted to know everything, powdering every conversation between Dave and me with questions. Dave had the innate ability (which I think comes with having a child) to tune out all but the important noise. "Is he crying? Is he hurt? Does this question need an answer?" I envied him.

I, on the other hand, heard and responded to *everything,* to my total exhaustion. I remember interrupting Ryan on one of his question-asking tirades, saying, "Why do you ask so many questions?"

His answer: "Because I'm five and I'm CUE-we-us!" Sigh.

But my fear of five-year-olds was nothing compared to my fear of meeting his mother. I was well aware that in many stepfamilies, "ex-wife" and "stepmother" are synonymous with the Wicked Witches of the Western Hemisphere. I couldn't imagine how one would "greet" the other without green venom spewing from their mouths. Ryan had proudly shown me his mom's picture, and I made a mental note that she didn't wear a pointy hat or ride a broom. In fact, as I told Ryan, she was beautiful. He beamed. I could see how much he loved her. That was great. But did I have to *meet* her?

The sudden, unexpected "meeting place" couldn't have been more emotionally charged. Dave's grandmother had died. And she—the *ex*—would be coming to the wake. Ryan, perfectly satisfied that Great Grandma was an angel now, had replaced his sorrow over her death with eagerness that his mother and I would finally have the chance to meet. But at a wake? Where's Emily Post when you need her?

I tried to blend into the walls of the funeral chapel, staying as inconspicuous as possible. But like a lioness defending her territory, I sensed when "she" arrived: the woman whom my husband's family had adopted first; the woman who'd given them a grandchild; the woman who would soon become a part of my life forever.

I watched her take Ryan by the hand and go to kneel by Great Grandma's casket. *Here's my chance,* I thought, *to escape.* The ladies' room. A chapel pew. Heck, an empty casket! Anything to avoid the inevitable.

I wasn't fast enough.

From my corner across the room, I saw what looked to be the parting of the Red Sea: a little boy making his way through the crowd of mourners, dragging his mother by the hand. "Mom! Mom!" I heard him say. "You've got to come meet Kris!" Oh, God. I saw fear scurry across her face after it twisted mine into the expression you get when you're about to throw up. I could feel everyone's eyes on us as we sized each other up like prizefighters before the bell went off. Would sparks fly? Would we implode upon impact? Would our heads spin around? No time to decide. Here she was.

"Mom, this is Kris. Kris, this is my Mom!"

Ryan's face was absolutely gleeful. Before she and I could exchange "not-so-niceties," he took her hand and tightly wrapped it around mine. As his father raced gallantly, although palely, to my side, Ryan then grabbed *his* hand and placed it on top of ours.

The silence was so thick, I expected a pin to drop and shatter it. Words eluded us—the grown-ups, that is. Because no sooner had we begun the polite struggle to pull away when, in one last burst of triumph, little Ryan stretched up and wrapped his little hands around all of ours.

"There!" he said. "Everybody I love is together!" His angel-face was elated. It was that simple.

And in that instant, the tension was gone. Here we "grown-ups" had been, with all of our societal and familial baggage, seeing only our differences and stereotypes, where a five-year-old angel had seen only love.

We smiled. "Sometimes it takes a child, doesn't it?" I said to his mom. She squeezed my hand and smiled. When love is the common ground, no one can be enemies. But it took a five-year-old angel to erase the battle lines.

"The Good Egg"

I've known my best friend Denise since high school. We went through everything together: boyfriends, Pom-Pon tryouts, summer jobs. What I've always loved about her is her hilarious honesty about life, including how ill-equipped she felt to be a mother. Forget Martha-Stewart-level domestic-goddess as an aspiration. Denise felt she'd be struggling to pull off a decent Roseanne Barr.

Then her little baby boy Orion came along: a miracle himself. Denise had been told long before that her severe endometriosis made it nearly impossible for her to have children. But there he was, and she loved being his mother. It was pretty easy at first, as babies have very few expectations (and have never watched Martha Stewart). But as we all know, kids get more demanding as they grow, and you don't want to be known as the neighborhood "slack-mom" during playground conversations. So when the annual Easter egg hunt was announced by the local Kiwanis club, she figured that was something she could do that would win her big brownie points with her young son. Or so she thought.

At three years old, Orion was thin and very blond. His angelic appearance mirrored his sweet demeanor. He was never prone to tantrums and seemed to have a level of understanding beyond his years. We girlfriends used to marvel out loud at the little boy's calm kindness, while silently we envied (translated "hated") Denise for her firstborn angel-child.

Anyway, it was the day before Easter, the day of the Big Easter Egg Hunt. Denise had been talking it up to Orion for days, and he was all excited, carrying his little wicker basket in anticipation of all the eggs he would find. The hunt was to begin promptly at ten, but when Denise got near the park, she found she had to park blocks away because of all the people who were there. As she and Orion walked toward the park, she noticed all the parents and their kids already walking *out of it*, carrying big bags of eggs.

It was only five after ten, Denise noted. But in her debut at Motherhood, she didn't know that kids and parents began lining up for the hunt at least an hour before it started, and by the time they were turned loose, no egg was safe for more than a few minutes.

Denise's heart began to sink as little Orion, oblivious to the big exodus of eggs, toddled along happily beside her. Desperately, Denise looked for any remaining eggs, any sign that perhaps another hunt was still going on for littler kids. But no such luck.

She knelt down beside him. "I am so sorry, Orion. It looks like we got here too late, and all the Easter eggs are gone."

Orion being Orion, there was no tantrum—not even a tear. This of course made Denise feel even worse, because she knew the downside to Orion's being so sweet and kind was that he got his feelings hurt very easily. She could see the disappointment in his eyes.

Then, out of the corner of her eye, Denise saw that a little boy had paused within hearing distance of her apology. He looked to be about nine years old with light-brown hair and freckles. He was wearing a dark-blue windbreaker, a light-blue T-shirt, jeans, and sneakers. In his hand he carried a big, white plastic bag, like the kind groceries come in, stuffed full of brightly-colored eggs.

Without saying a word, the boy took one of his eggs and placed it behind a tree. "Look!" He pointed so Orion could see. "I think there might be an egg over there!" Excitedly, Orion flew in his little toddler-run toward the tree and magically "found" an egg. Denise glanced at the boy who had placed it there, but he was already taking another egg from his bag and "hiding" it next to a rock. "Look!" he cried out again. "There might be another egg over there!" Orion gripped his tiny basket with one egg lolling around on the bottom and ran to the rock. "Look, Mama!" he said as he proudly held up the egg. "I found another one!" And on and on it went, with the nine-year-old boy quietly hiding the next egg while Orion gleamed over the one he'd just found. By the time Orion was finished, he had ten beautifully colored eggs in his basket.

After Denise helped Orion put the last egg in his basket, she stood up to thank the boy who had shared his treasure with her son. But the boy was nowhere to be seen. Little Orion was none the wiser that a nine-year-old stranger had appointed himself Orion's personal Easter Bunny and had saved Easter—not just for Orion but for a young mother whose one Easter wish was to make her son happy.

"Baby Bear"

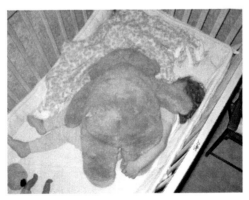

Two-year-old Sam vs. Teddy Bear. Teddy Bear wins.

At first I was just going to put this particular picture in my book because it's so danged funny. It's a picture of my daughter Sam when she was two, sleeping *underneath* her big teddy bear. We thought it looked like they'd been wrestling, and the bear had her in a full nelson. She slept on or under or over that bear every night when she was little. One night Dave said, "There's some kind of miracle here, something about 'wrestling with teddy bears' that belongs in your book." And that got me to thinking.

You know, if there's any lesson I've learned from Sam and my second daughter Alex, it's that the world can *always* be a new, exciting, and challenging place if you just look at it the way little kids do. Everything's bigger than you are, and even the good things in life can be intimidating: learning how to eat, ride a tricycle, and taking that first step into the kiddie pool. Yet day in and day out, little Sam and Alex always woke up with a smile and toddled into it all with anticipation and excitement.

Now, I'm not saying that every day's been a picnic. I mean, for God's sake, we're talking about toddlers here. Something as simple as having the wrong food put in front of them was cause for a meltdown. Oh, the draaaaaa-ma! They'd collapse on the floor in a puddle of snot and tears. Thirty seconds later, they'd be up dancing to Barney songs on the boom box. (Then *I'd* be the one who was crying!) Every emotion was so raw, so pure, so unedited. But kids just put them out there, get them out, and move on to the next adventure. And every night they seem to go to bed worn-out and happy with whatever the day has brought them.

Maybe that's what wrestling with teddy bears is all about. Sometimes even the best of things, the most comforting of things, can be challenging: a relationship, a job situation, a teddy bear that's bigger than you are. Maybe the trick is to just jump in the ring every day and wrestle that teddy bear the best you can, so that every night you can lie peacefully beside it (or under it, as the case may be) knowing that you've done your best and will wake up to a new day and fresh start in the morning. My girls do that really well. Maybe someday, if I'm a good student of theirs, so will I.

"Don't Sweat the Socks"

One late spring day, Dave and I were sitting in the kitchen, having just come in from playing ball with the kids. It had started to get a little chilly, so we thought we'd better bring our girls, who were toddlers at the time, inside. My stepson Ryan—being the eleven year old boy he was—was still out there messing around, oblivious to the cold, in his T-shirt and shorts.

We'd just gotten our sprinkler system turned on that day, so Dave decided to run it before dinner. He warned Ryan so that he wouldn't be caught off guard and get all wet. It turned out that for Ryan the warning was more like an invitation.

Suddenly a soggy blur began darting back and forth in front of the kitchen window—Ryan, running through the sprinklers in his T-shirt, shorts, and stocking feet.

Yes, he had given it enough thought to take off his shoes—but not his socks. (Huh?) Considering the amount of thought he gave to running through the sprinklers in the first place when it was maybe forty degrees outside with the sun going down, I guess the shoe thing was pretty impressive. But still ... *what was he thinking?*

Dave and I were about to run to the door and yell at him. (Oh, come on! You *know* you would too!) Scary visions of being in a detergent commercial—where I put one blackened sock in *ALL* and the other in *Tide* and both come out still dirty—shot through my mind. But as we watched, it became apparent that Ryan was having the time of his life: diving, leaping, and trying to second-guess where the water would spray next.

Unlike us old farts, he wasn't concerned with the minutiae of dirty socks, muddy tracks on the linoleum, or trying to make it from the doorway to the shower with the carpet somehow remaining unscathed.

He was *in the moment*, and we, sadly, were simply in the kitchen. I found myself laughing and humbled by Ryan's pure, uncomplicated joy. Like kids often do, he brought us back to our true selves, our fun selves, the selves we were when we used to do stuff just for the fun of it.

Later, I remembered that moment whenever my baby girls spit up on me after playing a fun game of tickle or chase. I *could* freak out about being covered in spit-up, *or* I could just enjoy being totally *in the moment* with my daughters, having a ball. After all, *they* were laughing, even with spit-up shooting out of their noses. If they could do it, if Ryan could do it, so could I!

"Yes! Debbie Does Daycare!"

Try being a TV news reporter and finding daycare. It'd be easier to find Jimmy Hoffa.

As a reporter, your work hours are either 10:00 a.m. to 6:30 p.m. or 2 p.m. to 10:30 p.m. And that's if you don't have any breaking news, which requires that you chase whoever did something wrong until either the police catch him or he holes up in some house and starts shooting at you. And that could take hours. Find a daycare that'll take *that* type of arrangement. I don't think so.

That was a part of having a baby that I never anticipated. It's not like news people don't have babies. I mean, didn't Joan Lunden have about fourteen of them while she was on Good Morning America? Of course, she made enough money to hire a nanny, so I guess it's not *exactly* the same. And she wasn't married to a news photographer who had the same crappy hours. So when Sam was born, Dave and I were in a fix.

We went through the county to get a list of all licensed daycare centers. No center was open after 5:30, with the exception of one thirty-five miles away that the air traffic controllers at the Minneapolis-St. Paul International Airport used, and another at Mall of America next to Camp Snoopy. Imagine dropping your infant off at a place that sounded like a carnival and had views of screaming kids on Ferris wheels!

So, we turned reluctantly to a listing of in-home daycare providers. I say *reluctantly* because Dave and I had done way too many stories about in-home daycares where something creepy or tragic happened to the kids. But even the majority of potentially creepy daycare providers didn't have the hours we needed. That left us with about eight to choose from. I told Dave that I would start calling.

So a few days later, I got out the list again. One name kept jumping out at me: "Debbie's Daycare." Now, it didn't have any more "bells and whistles" than the rest of them. Her hours were seven to seven. She had a separate play area, fenced-in yard, two dogs, etc. So I kept looking. But my eyes (and gut) always wound up back at Debbie's. So I dialed.

I got voicemail. Which I thought could be a good thing, since she was probably teaching the children a second language or geometry or Sanskrit and didn't want to disrupt the lesson. Or it could be a bad thing because she'd finally had enough and locked herself in a closet and left the baby gate open so the kids could tumble to their deaths in the basement. I left a brief message and my number, somewhat relieved that she didn't answer.

I still didn't call anyone else.

Pretty soon the phone rang and it was Debbie, sounding out-of-breath but happy, with kids squealing (but not crying, I noted) in the background. "So ... (pant-pant) you need daycare for your baby (pant)?"

"Yes, but I have crazy hours. I work at Channel 5 ..."

"Channel 5? Oh! Do you know Jim Biaggi?"

"Well, yes ... he's our live truck operator. A good friend of ours ..."

"Oh, Jim's like family. I've been taking care of his two kids since they were six weeks old." (His kids were then 5 and 6.)

"But the crazy hours ..."

"Oh, I *know* all about his crazy news hours. Sometimes they'd send him up to Brainerd, and I'd have to keep his kids overnight. No problem ... just give me a call."

"Really?"

"Oh, yah." (Debbie was definitely Minne-*sooo*-tan). "Noooo problem. Really." I couldn't have been more in disbelief if Mary Poppins had just flown in on her parasol.

So we arranged a time for us to go over and interview her. In the meantime, we would check her out with our good friend Jim.

Now, Jim's a burly, friendly Italian guy, who knows everybody in Minneapolis and St. Paul, and all the police love him and let him park his live truck just about anywhere he wants. Jim is "good people," and if he likes someone, you know they're the real deal.

Debbie, he raved, was the real deal. His kids thought of her as family. He trusted Debbie implicitly, as well as her daughters who regularly babysat. And his crazy hours were never a problem. You just had to call and let her know.

And the moment we met Debbie, we knew too. It was that gut feeling that most of us don't pay attention to enough, and this gut feeling was practically a kick. Debbie, who was just a little older than we were, was the mother of two college-aged girls and had been doing daycare since she'd had the first one some twenty-two years earlier.

She had been named Daycare Provider of the County two years before. But what I noticed most about her was that she was *normal*. Her house was comfortably messy; you could tell that kids played there and that she didn't freak when the Oreos wound up smeared on the wall or the couch got jumped on.

Here and there we saw an abandoned shoe or sock, purposefully left where it landed so its owner could come back and find it the next day. There were classic toys: blocks, puzzles, table and chairs, rattles, dolls, a mini kitchen, and games. Nothing too high-tech. Kids had to use their imaginations. And her wall upstairs was decorated with kids' pictures and the things they had made for her. She had a great, loud laugh and a playful way about her. Her shirt wasn't tucked in. Her hair was gathered haphazardly behind her ears as if some baby had just pulled it. She crouched down on the floor, eye-level with Sam, and made her laugh. We loved her. And for the next several years, she would love our kids like they were her own.

Sam is now eight, and her little sister Alex is six-and-a-half. Even though Dave and I have normal jobs now and the girls are in school, they still talk about Debbie and her girls like they're family. They learned so much from her and the other kids—like potty-training, thank you very much, and how to play well with others. We have boxes of crafts they brought home from Debbie's, many of which were covered with applesauce or cookies or whatever they'd managed to smear on their faces and hair that day. They couldn't have been happier. Neither could we.

After all of our grief and worry over trying to find daycare, we found an angel in Debbie: a loving, fun, spit-up-covered angel. I thank God every day for that "gut feeling" I got when I saw her name on the list, and for the fact that I actually followed it.

But most of all, I thank God that Debbie *does* daycare!

"TGIF (on Monday)"

It was one of those days when suddenly I looked at the clock and it was four in the afternoon—and the only measure of what I'd done all day was the number of dirty diapers I'd changed and the artistic trail of snotty Kleenexes that lay scattered throughout the house. I hadn't even showered yet. I felt grimy and goo'ed-upon and wholly unappreciated by my poopy and snotty baby girls. I was sure that the whole more-exciting adult world was passing me by.

And it was only Monday.

Mercifully, my husband Dave called on his way home from work and suggested that we take the kids out for dinner. We chose TGI Friday's for their family-friendly atmosphere—or what I like to call "Distractions Are Us": bright colors, crayons with menus to color in, even a balloon guy who goes around to every kid and makes them a balloon animal. Oh, and the fact that they served really cold beer didn't hurt either.

My stepson Ryan, who was eleven at the time, was giving us his usual play-by-play of the entire school day without taking a breath; two-year-old Sam was immersed in the physics of drinking from a straw; and baby Alex was happily hanging out in her car seat that we'd placed in one of those slings that restaurants have. There was really nothing remarkable about the scene; or so I thought.

After we ordered, our server came up with a gift card and said, "That couple over there thought you had such a nice family and such well-behaved kids that they wanted to pick up some of your dinner tonight." My husband and I looked over to where she pointed: an elderly couple in a booth diagonally behind us. We couldn't see the woman's face because her back was to us, but she had old-lady gray hair and was wearing a sweater that looked lovingly knit by hand; her husband, whose face we could see, was wearing a plaid, flannel old-man shirt, buttoned all the way to the top. And his grandpa-type face had lots of smile wrinkles around the eyes and mouth. He was cutely hunched like some old men get, as if they're in a permanent happy shrug. But he never looked up at us after we got their gift card—just sat there sipping his after-dinner coffee and chatting quietly with his wife.

Ryan managed to take a breath and insert, "Hey, I could get one of those gummy-worm mud-pie desserts with the gift card!" and then went on about who ran fastest at recess. Then Sam tried to dunk the gift card in her milk. As Dave and I swam over the table from one kid to the next, trying to keep anything from spilling, I saw the old couple slowly walking toward the door. I motioned to Dave, who in one stroke had rescued the gift card and smoothly slipped it in his pocket without Sam seeing where it went. She sat open-mouthed and amazed. Then Dave stood up and offered his hand to the man as we thanked them profusely for their kindness. The grandpa barely looked up from his hunchy shuffle and gruffly waved it off, like we must have the wrong guy. His wife, who had grandma-glasses and the kind of hairdo that you can only get at a beauty parlor, just smiled. She said, "It's just nice to see such a beautiful family."

And with that, they were gone. After they left, the restaurant manager came up and said, "They come here every Monday night at the same time and sit in the exact same booth. And every Monday they watch for a family to treat—a family they think deserves it."

I looked around our table. Ryan had politely thanked the people in the midst of his narrative but otherwise hadn't come up for air. I looked over at Sam, noticing the playful curls at the nape of her neck as she rearranged the coasters on the table again and again. And baby Alex was fast asleep, sucking from an imaginary bottle. My husband, my co-creator of this family, was sitting across from me, smiling, his eyes shining.

It was then that I realized my "accomplishments" were much bigger than wiping butts and noses all day. They were sitting there all around me. My "worth" shone in the happy, contented eyes of the people I loved. And the "more exciting adult world" (that elderly couple) seemed to think I was doing a damned good job.

And at last, at that moment, so did I.

"Tooting His Own Horn"

It wasn't until school was about to start that Ryan informed us he was taking up band. Not that this was a bad thing. It's just that he was already signed up for Geography Club and Academic Team and something called Destination Imagination. Visions of carpools and early mornings trampled through our heads. So did the assorted noises of musical instruments he could choose from. (Please, God, don't let it be the drums!)

Not wanting to discourage him from music altogether, we said, "How about choir?" Nope. All of his friends were joining band. Which meant, of course, that *he* was joining band.

Well, it being so late for this well-thought-out decision, Ryan found out that the only instruments left to be chosen in the band were the trumpet and the trombone. The whole "sliding arm" deal on the trombone fascinated Ryan to no end, so off we went to the music store to rent the thing. Unfortunately, he couldn't wait until his first lesson to "play" it for us. We spent that night wincing between smiles, a captive audience to his eager squawks and twister-like contortions, all the while trying to keep our sixteen-month-old Sam from screaming in fear.

Between our house and Ryan's mom's house, the "practicing" wasn't too bad. He actually played something resembling "Jingle Bells" at Christmas. It kind of sounded like Charlie Brown's teacher, for those of you familiar with her "voice." Hauling the trombone back and forth was a pain. Every Wednesday, it was "bang-bang-bang" as he made it out the door and into the van. Bang-bang-bang as he unloaded it for school.

Thank goodness it was in a case. Then it was bang-bang-bang again as he brought it back home. Then, of course, squawk-squawk-squawk, etc.

To my surprise, when we went to his last band concert of the year, the trombone section (Ryan and one other kid) was on tune and on tempo. Whereas I'd only planned on staying for one or two songs—my excuse being that our two babies (Alex had been born that December) needed to go to bed, I wound up staying for and enjoying the whole thing. I began thinking that the whole trombone adventure might have been worth it after all.

Until Ryan informed us that he wanted to buy one. He said he planned on playing in junior high next year, so why not buy one so he could practice *all summer*? Suddenly I had flashes of having to keep our windows closed all summer, with angry neighbors outside on their lawns.

Dave had a quick, understandable answer. "It's too expensive," Dave told Ryan. And besides, maybe Ryan would want to try some other instrument by the time school started again. If not, they could talk about "buying one" then.

Ryan only offered one "but Daaaaaaad ..." in argument. Disappointed, he decided that he still wanted to go with Dave to return his trombone to the music store. With a heavy heart, he bang-bang-banged it for the last time unloading it from the van, with one more bang for good measure as he went through the music store doorway. Dave took it from there.

Ryan began looking around for something to occupy himself while Dave finalized the paperwork. And there it was. Over in the corner, propped up and dusty, stood an old trombone case with a sign leaning against it that said "FREE." Ryan couldn't believe his eyes. He ran over to it. Not only was it a trombone case, but there was an actual trombone inside!

"Daaaaaad! Daaaaaad!" Dave shushed him for a moment while he finished up. "But Daaaaaad!" When Dave finally looked, it was with that familiar parental mixture of "Great!" versus "Oh, great." A *free* trombone. Where was the argument now? He checked with the store owner. Yes, an elderly gentleman had just stopped by the store, asking whether they could use it to rent to the kids. The store owner had told him the trombone was too old to rent out or sell. So the old man simply said, Well, put a sign on it that says "free," and whoever sees it or wants it can have it.

Then Ryan came in.

That night, Ryan took out the old trombone like a prize treasure he'd found; he assembled the tarnished slide arm and wiggled the mouthpiece into place (after we'd disinfected it for about half an hour with hot water and antibacterial soap). He plopped down on the floor with some of his old music and began to play.

It was so good that Dave and I found ourselves humming along, and two-year-old Sam began to dance. Baby Alex smiled.

This may have been Ryan's miracle, but it was one that touched all of us and taught us a lesson.

"Mothers' (Very Long) Day"

Pregnancies usually last about nine months. This is the story of one that lasted more than nineteen and required four mothers, two languages and thousands of miles (and dollars) to bring one baby boy home.

It's about my good friend Lorri, whom I met while working at KSTP. I can remember clearly the first time Lorri walked by my desk. It was right after she got hired: the new photojournalist phenom from Phoenix. I remember because, in the midst of the din that is a newsroom – phones ringing, assignment managers yelling, reporters yelling back, and photographers running out the door loaded up with gear, Lorri came up to me with a warmth and laid-back southern charm that was anything *but* frantic and self-important. When we were introduced, she looked me in the eye and smiled a full-body smile, the kind that comes from the heart. She seemed truly surprised and humbled that she had been chosen out of a field of many as the most talented candidate for the job. This of course made her the perfect candidate, not only for the job but also for a lifelong friend.

Early on, during one of our many long days in the news van, I learned that one of Lorri's dreams in life was to become a mother. She told me that during high school, while other kids vied for jobs at McDonalds and Pizza Hut and the Gap, she had gone to work (for much less money) at a daycare. When her sister had kids, Lorri practically forced her and her husband to go out so she could babysit. And when her sister would return from wherever she'd been, Lorri would be just as giggly and messy and happy as her nieces and nephews. Lorri had even had a dream about a little baby girl named Emily, who she believed would be her daughter someday. It was clear that Lorri had the heart of a mother.

But life wasn't going to make it easy for Lorri. As a lesbian, Lorri faced the obvious obstacles—whether she wanted to conceive or adopt. She and her partner Misty had been together nearly a decade, complete with a commitment ceremony; but in the eyes of the law, they were not optimal adoption material. So they decided to save their money and try artificial insemination, hoping that Lorri could conceive and bring them the child they so longed for. But thousands of dollars and dozens of fertilization procedures later, Lorri still wasn't pregnant. At age forty-one, her dream was running out of time.

They decided to try adoption. Agencies told them that adopting from another country was probably the fastest way for them to get a baby, but that many countries were reluctant to adopt to same-sex couples. So, either Lorri or Misty would have to adopt as a single mom. When Lorri and Misty asked about requesting a girl, the agency said it would be better to mark "either" on the sex preference in order to expedite their application. Like all parents, their primary wish was for a healthy baby. Girl vs. boy was secondary. So they said yes and officially began trying to "conceive" through a maze of paperwork, references, home visits, and payments.

Unlike a traditional pregnancy, there were no signs of the life they hoped to bring into their world. No ultrasounds, fluttery kicks, or morning sickness. There was the occasional call from the adoption agency to clarify some information and update them on the process. But all in all, Lorri and Misty sat in a vacuum of waiting, graciously celebrating the births of their friends' children (including ours) without any clue as to when—if ever—they would be doing the same. Months went by. Their silent phone and empty mailbox were becoming unbearable, so they decided to take their lives off "hold" and go visit Misty's father in Prescott, Arizona. It was then that they got the call.

The agency told them about a three-week-old baby boy from Guatemala. His young, unwed mother already had several children and could not afford another. The baby was going into foster care. Were they interested? The agency e-mailed them a picture. And when they saw his little, round face with inky-black eyes, they knew. This was their child. Not "Emily" but "Emilio" or Milo for short. They said yes, and once again, the waiting began.

They exchanged photos with Milo's foster mom. They sent him clothing and presents. Every two months or so, their agent would visit Guatemala and return with a video of their little boy—tiny and toothless but always smiling as if to say, *Here I am, waiting for you!*

But the process took forever: documents and language barriers, trying to find the father to make sure he was giving up his parental rights, a mother who was hard to track down because of her impoverished status. Every roadblock raised the fear in Lorri's heart that Milo could be taken away.

Then in March, one year after he was born, they got word. Just six more weeks and they could come get him. Just like any prospective parents on the eve of childbirth, they were excited and terrified. But unlike most prospective parents' circumstances, their "hospital" was Guatemala, and their OB nurse was Milo's foster mom who had grown to love him like her own. How would the delivery go? And how would Milo react to his moms?

But their fears dissolved the moment they saw him. Misty says she can't imagine loving any baby more—like he had always been a part of them. And Milo seemed to feel the same way, to the point where Lorri and Misty worried whether something was wrong with him because he never cried. He simply ate, played, and slept, soaking up the love of two mothers.

Lorri and Misty spent ten days in Guatemala with Milo, hoping to understand at least a little of his culture before they brought him home. Like most new mothers, those first days were a blur. But the significance of their long "pregnancy" with Milo and his eventual homecoming was not lost on them—or on those of us who loved them.

That's why we gathered at the airport: my best friend Sharon and I (Sharon had come to know and love Lorri and Misty too) and our husbands and kids. We anxiously waited with signs and balloons to welcome Milo home the way Lorri and Misty had celebrated our kids' homecomings. And at long last, there they were, gingerly pushing their previously empty stroller—now full of Milo and all things baby—down the concourse. That in itself would have made the day special. But it just so happened that this day—after all the paperwork and waiting and preparation and hoping—this day when God and the courts and whatever other powers-that-be allowed Lorri and Misty to come home and begin their lives as Milo's moms, was, in fact, Mother's Day, 2004.

"Truth or D.A.R.E."

It was one of those school programs that, as a parent, you just *know* will go on and on, only to see your kid for five or ten seconds at the end getting handed some certificate, giving you a sheepish don't-make-a-scene grin, and then hurrying back to class.

It was my stepson Ryan's graduation from "D.A.R.E.," the program that teaches kids how and why to stay away from drugs. I felt I had to go, since my husband was out of town for work and Ryan's mom had an important meeting to go to. My own excuse was only a terrible sleep deficit due to being home alone with two babies who refused to sleep at the same time, leaving me a walking zombie. (Come to think of it, that was probably the perfect time to attend one of these!)

The graduation was being held in the gymnasium that doubled as the auditorium, with us parents seated comfortably (yeah, right) in creaky, metal folding chairs. Those fluorescent lights that must be made especially for school gymnasiums were making everyone look pale and tired. Or maybe it was just me. And of course the thing wasn't starting on time, so the usual hum that happens when strangers feel compelled to break an uncomfortable silence began to set in. The man in front of me happily turned around and introduced himself. He was the father of one of Ryan's friends. He was a big guy, which made his sitting on that tiny folding chair pretty hilarious. But I was very touched by his presence, because he'd gone to work early, then saved his lunch hour just so he could be there for the ten seconds his son was going to spend at the podium getting his certificate.

We started up a fun conversation about parenthood and its trials and tribulations.

His two sons were nearly three years apart, and while he empathized with my lack of sleep from having my girls just eighteen months apart, he said he wished he had had his boys closer together—one reason, so they'd be better friends than rivals, and two, because of the lesson the second one taught him—the lesson that made him a better father.

He said at first he couldn't imagine having more than one child, because you give that first child everything you have—all of your energy, your time, and all of your heart. How could there possibly be any love left for another? But when son number two came along, there it was. All the love, all the joy, and all the awesome feelings he'd had for son number one, doubled. He learned then that the more love he gave, the more he had—love he could lavish on both boys while being a better father to them.

He said he always tells people now that his second son taught him what love was really all about.

I thought about my girls and how I'd been dreading this week alone with them while Dave was out of town—the lack of sleep, the tantrums, the one crying while I tended to the needs of the other. I had been feeling overwhelmed, crabby, and more dutiful than joyful. Ryan's graduation had also seemed like a huge imposition. All of it had. Until now.

As Ryan approached the podium to receive his certificate, I took the obligatory parent photo, and then waited afterward to have him pose with his friend so I could take another one. He asked me when I'd gotten there because he hadn't seen me until then. I said I'd been there the whole time and had seen the whole thing. He smiled.

And as he hurried down the hall back to his class, I thought of that father's timely words about love and how the more love you give away, the more you have.

"Hey, Ryan," I called after him. "Can I give you a hug?"

This could have been his worst nightmare, there in front of all his friends. It could easily be grounds for expulsion from the "cool kids club." And then I would officially be the Stepmother from Hell.

I waited.

Ryan turned around, and there, right in front of everybody, he came up and gave *me* a hug.

"Thanks, Kris," he said. And I noticed that the cool kids were still waiting for him as he left my side. Funny thing about love, I learned that day. The more you give away the more you have. I guess I was the one who really needed to go to school that day.

"Routine Matters"

It was the end of the day on a Monday, and already Dave's and my work-week routine was in full swing, hopefully productive, and capped off by bringing the girls home from daycare. The usual chaos ensued: Sam was locked into the phrase, "Mama, I want some *jooooos!*" like a record with dust in its grooves. Baby Alex had a good case of the squirms, in which she arches against the straps of her car seat so hard that her resulting groans ripen her little round head the shade of a tomato. Without a word, Dave freed her and swept her upstairs for a new diaper (the need for which is often a cause of the squirms).

Just as routinely, I de-velcroed Sam's shoes and settled her down, legs kicking, into one of the kitchen chairs and inserted "You-have-to-have-some-din-ner" in between her repeated "I want some *jooooos!*" Up-down-up-down-up-down in the chair she went, still chanting, while I quickly slathered some peanut butter on a slice of bread and cut it diagonally down the middle, which she seemed to think made it "funner" to eat. Before she could utter *jooooos* one more time, I whirled around, whisking a new sippy-cup from the cupboard and pouring milk into it to take its place next to the peanut butter sandwich. I was getting quite good at this quick combo, and it usually slowed her down long enough for me to come up with some version of fruit or vegetable to sneak in beside it before she remembered her *jooooos.*

I can't remember what sides I drummed up; they always wound up in some melting pot of a concoction somewhere near her plate. But I do remember plopping down in the chair next to her as she chattered nonsensically at her sandwich, thinking that the five or so minutes she'd be busy wiping the peanut butter from ear to ear—with the occasional score into the mouth—would be a welcome respite from the chaos and routine of parenthood.

I reached for the remote and turned on the news, as I always did while Sam "did her thing." Suddenly Sam stopped chattering and looked at the TV. Then at me. Then at the TV again. "No, Mama! *No!*" she said.

"What?" I was surprised she'd come up for air and even noticed. "Why?"

"No, Mama! Talk to *meeeeee!*"

This certainly was not part of the routine. I was so taken aback that I promptly pushed the red on/off button on the remote and pushed it far away from me on the table. "Okay, Sam." I said. "What should we talk about? Let's see ..."

It didn't matter. "Did you have fun at daycare today? Who was there? What did you have for lunch? Was Baby Alex good today?" and on and on. The "conversation" was mostly mine, with her happily nodding or shaking her head as peanut butter and crumbs danced from her upper lip to her bottom one.

That moment has stuck with me. To Sam, to Alex, coming home and being with us was not and never has been "routine." It's not something they take for granted or simply go through the motions of on their way to bed. The *jooooooos*, the diaper changes, the mindless—or what I previously thought was mindless—chatter ... it's all special.

I just needed a two-year-old to tell me to turn off the TV and pay attention.

"Guitar Lessons"

I started playing the guitar in sixth grade, envisioning my future fame as a country singer like Patsy Cline, Anne Murray, and Crystal Gayle. My lessons came courtesy of our neighbor down the street, Gerry Way, who was a music teacher and played in his own band on weekends. He was an accomplished guitarist, but my instrumental aspirations were not that high. I simply wanted a way to accompany my singing until I became famous enough to have someone else play *for* me.

So practicing really wasn't my deal. No matter how much my parents encouraged me to play and perform for them, I learned just enough to get by. It was good enough to help me win the Miss Chippewa Valley Pageant when I was a senior in high school. But other than that, I viewed the guitar as a temporary necessity.

So why did I take it with me everywhere I moved over the next twenty years? From time to time my mom would ask me, "Do you *ever* play the guitar anymore?" knowing that I didn't, followed by, "Oh, I don't know *why* you don't play anymore. You were *so good.*" Which of course, even at age thirty-eight, made me *not* want to play it even more. Still, I held on to the damned thing, never knowing why.

Enter my stepson, Ryan. For years he played the games little boys play in the shadow of my guitar, stopping long enough, once in a while, to listen to my half-hearted attempts to appease my mom. Then he'd be off again … with Dave at his busy little heels, trying to figure out what sport his little boy was going to be good at. Baseball? Not interested. Basketball? Ryan dutifully trotted up and down the court but was just as happy sitting on the bench. Football? Dave was hard-pressed to get Ryan to throw the ball even a few times in the yard. It soon became obvious that he had fathered something other than a sports phenom. But what?

Then one day, after years of dabbling in karate, theater, and band, Ryan picked up my guitar—my old, dusty, resented guitar. He picked it up like he'd held it for years, cradling its neck in his left hand, hugging it under his right arm. I was tempted to roll my eyes, anticipating my mother's next generation of "Why don't you/he ever play anymore?" I heard him play first one string, then the next. Like he knew them. Minutes went by, then hours. Ryan couldn't put it down. Neither Dave nor I said a word, as time and time again Ryan would come home from school, put down his books, and pick up the guitar. He taught himself to play and how to read music, and not long after, he left traditional songs behind to create his own, blues-y style of original music.

It turned out that Ryan was and is a natural guitarist, good enough to get into the St. Paul Conservatory for the Performing Arts, a high school dedicated to talented musicians. He gets asked to jam with local bands, and he composes music for some of Dave's videos. And even though he's since invested in a number of newer models, he still defaults to my old guitar, making it sing like it never did in my own hands.

My mom has since passed away; but I derive some comfort in being able to tell her—and myself—that my guitar lessons did result in some amazing music being played to this day: that of my stepson's.

"Cue Card"

When my daughter Sam was about eight months old, I got a job as a reporter and producer for a national production company. It was a really good set-up because I worked out of my home. But after the birth of my second daughter Alex and the lack of any work colleagues other than my husband, I found myself falling into the occasional stay-at-home-mom rut in that what-I-do-doesn't-count-for-much frame of mind.

Now, I *do* know better. I know that motherhood is the toughest—and ultimately the most important—job I'll ever have. But when you feel isolated and stupidly tired and feel like the rest of the world is doing something far more interesting than you … well, you get in a rut.

So one night after I had put Alex to bed and Dave had taken Sam to Ryan's baseball practice, I decided to take out one of my cardboard boxes filled with memorabilia from my former, non-mom life—just to prove that I'd had one. I don't know if I just wanted to be a glutton for punishment, indulge my depression, or what. Maybe it was just to keep me from eating a pint of Haagen Dazs.

Beneath some of my journals and celebrity autographs that I'd garnered over the years, I found a plain, paper-maché-like card that said only, "Muchas Gracias from John, Katie, and Fern." Inside was a picture of me surrounded by children in Cali, Colombia. It was from a story I had done back in '98 about a team of American doctors and nurses who went there to perform heart surgeries for needy children. It had been one of most eye-opening, heart-wrenching experiences I'd ever had. John, Katie, and Fern had headed up the charity that organized the mission.

On the back of the card was a simple saying but one that I sorely needed right then. It said:

"A hundred years from now, it will not matter what my bank account was, the sort of house I lived in, or the kind of car I drove, but the world may be different because I was important in the life of a child."

I thought of Sam and Alex. How they smiled and wiggled when they saw me. How they clung to me for hugs and comfort.

Suddenly my "nothing" role meant everything. And I was reminded that, if this is "all" I do in life, being Sam's and Alex's mom, it'll make all the difference in the world.

I keep that card right by my computer now to remind me that even a so-called mom-rut can really be the path of all hope, for all time.

How to See Miracles as a Parent

One of our favorite photos of our daughter, Sam. It reminds
us that with parenting, really, it's *all* good.

For a crash course in how to see miracles as a parent, I went to
Dr. Marti Erickson, founding director of the Children, Youth, and
Family Consortium and, more recently, director of the Irving B. Harris
Programs and co-chair of the University of Minnesota President's
Initiative on Children, Youth and Families. If you want a breath of
fresh air about real-life parenting skills—the kind you need when you
haven't had a shower in three days and your toddler looks at you like
she can't believe she got *you* as a mom—Marti's the best. She and her
daughter Erin host a brutally honest, reassuring, and very useful weekly
podcast called "Mom Enough™" (www.MomEnough.com) that can
pull just about any frantic parent back from the edge.

To see miracles in our kids, Marti says, we first have to lighten up
on *ourselves*. Society's pressure to be uber-parents only gets in the way of
recognizing and experiencing what really matters. View yourself with
compassion. We each have our own parenting baggage from our moms
and dads; we each have our own inherent strengths and weaknesses.
So instead of striving to keep up with "the Joneses of parenting" (and
what makes *them* the experts, anyway?), strive to be the best *you* can be
at parenting *your* kids. Know what your triggers and weaknesses are.
Learn to offset them as best you can. And don't expect yourself to be
perfect.

Second, teach yourself the art of the time-out. Parents need them
just like kids do. When sweet little Ashley gets on your very last nerve,
take a break. Remove yourself from the meltdown and practice some

deep breathing. It won't necessarily change the situation, but it will give you the perspective to deal with it more calmly and from a better place—often with better results.

Marti herself is a big fan of taking "nature breaks." Get the little ones outdoors to burn off steam and to take advantage of the many distractions nature offers. She even carries two folding chairs in the trunk of her car for the occasional "in-transit meltdowns" with her grandkids. She simply pulls over to a nearby park or grassy area, gets out the chairs, and gets the unhappy child out of the car seat to breathe some fresh air with Grandma and maybe check out a bug or two. She says it works like magic, not only for the little ones, but for Grandma as well.

Finally, Marti encourages us to learn as much about child development as we can. She's not necessarily talking about checking out textbooks from the local library or taking a community ed class (although by all means, if you have the time and the interest, please go ahead). This actually can be as easy as Googling "child development at age 5" or visiting a parenting website. Another resource she recommends is "Minnesota Parents Know," a state-funded website packed with written information and audio and video clips to help parents learn about typical child development and also to guide them in where to turn if they have concerns that their child's development is not on track. Finding out what's normal for your child at a particular age and reminding yourself how he or she sees the world right then helps us understand their often curious and sometimes maddening behavior.

The coolest thing about kids is that they haven't forgotten how to see—and appreciate—miracles in the everyday. They see the world through innocent eyes. No expectations. No baggage. Everything about their world is new and exciting. They immerse themselves in the adventure of not knowing what's next. This is how to see miracles. So cherish the chance to get down on your knees with your kid and really look at that ant carrying a bread crumb four times its size. See the world through your child's eyes. It really is quite amazing.

Chapter Three: Job Miracles

Being in TV News Is Kind of Like Being a Parent.

You love it and you hate it, all at the same time. There's the adrenaline rush of covering breaking news but also the danger, long hours, and low pay that often go along with it. One moment you feel great because your story helped someone in some way; the next you feel like crap because someone slammed a door in your face simply because you're "the media."

I've had bosses who have made me cry, and I've been laid off twice—most recently when (perfect timing) I had just begun writing this chapter. (I told God I didn't think that was funny.) Laid off—with three kids, a mortgage, and a financed minivan. But writing this chapter was just what I needed to keep believing that a job miracle was on its way. And it was. My kids didn't starve. We've still got our minivan, and although I hate minivans, at least we're not having to live out of it. And I've landed at a job that I absolutely love.

At a time when unemployment is high—and Americans are changing jobs an average of seven to ten times during their lives——job miracles can be hard to see. But I promise you, they're there.

As you read these stories, you'll find that no job has to be viewed as a mistake or a waste of time and that actually finding the miracle in your own situation can be your first step toward making it better.

It is my hope that "Job Miracles" will do for you what it's done for me and the other people in these stories: keep you believing in the American Dream.

"The Voice of Doom"

So there I was, twenty-seven years old, sitting on the floor in my office in Chicago, sobbing. I had curled myself into a ball in the corner between my pink filing cabinet and the exposed brick wall, wanting to just disappear. I at least had the presence of mind to close and lock the door before my meltdown, but my office was the kind that had no ceiling (it was in a rehabbed warehouse), so I had the nearly impossible task of stuffing down a full-out sobbing fit without making any noise. I remember doing that gasping thing that kids do when they're crying hard and trying to talk at the same time, the hot tears running down my face, mixing with the snot from my nose, and dropping into my mouth. Yum. Yeah, it was a good day at work.

How did I get to this lovely place? Well, rewind to earlier that day. I was working as a fairly successful writer/producer at a production company downtown. But of course my ultimate dream was to be an on-air, television news reporter. So, when my boss Jeff asked me if I'd like to audition to narrate one of our videos that afternoon, I was elated, thinking this could be my big break. (Even though you wouldn't actually *see* me on the tape—just hear my voice—it was something.)

So I got a copy of the script, and I practiced and practiced and practiced. I enunciated. I projected. I did my best Barbara Walters imitation (without the lisp). So when it came time to go into the sound booth and record, I felt pretty good about my chances. I put on the headphones, and Jeff said to me from the recording booth, "Okay, whenever you're ready. Rolling!" I took a deep breath and began to read. My heart sounded louder than my voice to me, but I didn't stumble or anything. So when Jeff interrupted me after only about thirty seconds, I was surprised.

"Uh, Patrow ... start again from the top. Let's have it a little more conversational, with a little more inflection. Okay, rolling!"

I wasn't quite sure what he meant, but I made a mental note to make my pitch go up and down a little more. I certainly was projecting enough. And my mother would have been proud of how crisp my consonants were. (I know that's weird, but you'd have to know my mom. She was a librarian and really got into things like that.) So I started again.

And in ten seconds, he stopped me again.

"Okay, Patrow? Patrow. Relax. Just take a deep breath, slow it down, and let's hear more variety in your read. One more time, from the top ..."

I've always hated it when people tell me to relax. It only confirms to me that I am not handling something well, which makes me even more keyed-up. I even told my husband Dave not to say that word when I was delivering our daughter. "I don't care what you do, just *don't* say *relax*." So when he did, I think my head spun around mid-push and did the exorcist thing on him. He's never said it since.

Back to the story.

Telling me to relax and do better when I already thought I was doing my best only made me more nervous. But I started again, trying so hard to sound different, better. This time, after about twenty seconds, Jeff simply walked into the sound booth. I jumped, because I had my headphones on and didn't hear him coming. I thought he was coming to fix some technical problem. Turns out, he was coming in to fix *me*.

I can still see him, looking down as if the words he wanted to say were somewhere on the floor. The top of his head was balding, I noted. He kicked at some imaginary something on the carpet with his sneaker. After a big breath, he looked up at me and said: "Patrow, I'm not saying this to hurt your feelings. But it's better you find this out now, sooner than later. Patrow, you have the absolute *worst* voice I've ever heard. It's high-pitched, it's monotone, and you've got this sing-songy way of talking. There's *no* way you can ever be a news reporter or have a career in broadcasting. I'm sorry, I know it's your dream, but you've got to face reality."

I could see his mouth moving, but his words were on like a two-second delay as I tried to process what he was saying. *No* career in broadcasting. *Worst* voice he'd ever heard. It wasn't like I had a zit or the wrong haircut or was too fat—all things I could change. It was my *voice*. I suddenly felt sick and hot and like I couldn't breathe. I just wanted to get away from Jeff as fast as possible so he couldn't see me cry. Somehow I squeaked out an "okay ..." and did my best nonchalant walk to my office.

I lightly shut the door, pushed the lock, and made a beeline for the corner on the floor. I had a lot to process, considering my dream had just been decimated.

First, I felt humiliated. I respected Jeff *so* much, and there I was, reading in my stupid voice in front of him—so badly that he felt compelled to come in and *make* me stop. Second, I felt like someone had died. Specifically, me. All these years I'd had it in my mind that I would be a television news reporter. That's what I'd told everyone. That's what I'd told my skeptical first husband who thought I'd just get over it someday and be content to be his seen-but-not-heard domestic goddess. Now, the tether that tied me to my future had been cut. Butchered. I was flailing out there in twenty-something land with no direction and no map.

So I sat there, feeling sorry for myself and sobbing off all of my makeup. One of my whimpers must have leapt over the wall, because all of a sudden Jeff was at my door, knocking.

"Patrow, you all right?"

"J-J-Jess."

"Can I come in?"

"Doe."

I didn't want to see the Voice of Doom. Hell, I especially didn't want him to see me like that. I don't remember what he said, but I remember thinking: God, just *stop talking. Stop stop stop.* I didn't want to hear any more about my other "options" out there. I just wanted to feel shitty.

So finally I convinced him not to scale the wall of my office, to just leave. By then, it was the end of the workday. So I waited until almost everyone had left, and then I scurried out, eyes down. The last thing I wanted to do was talk to someone so they could hear my stupid voice.

I don't remember at what point I got pissed-off enough about what Jeff had said to start sending out my resume and tape anyway. Jeff's words were like a two-year-old saying the same thing over and over again until he finally convinces you to do what he wants, *now.* Jeff thought I was a terrific writer and producer. He thought I'd have a terrific career behind the scenes. He thought I'd be happy with that.

He was wrong.

So when the unimaginable happened and I got an offer from the NBC affiliate in Champaign, Illinois, I broke into a gleeful I-told-you-so dance all the way to work. Happily, I wrote up my resignation and left it on Jeff's desk.

So I wasn't surprised when over the pager I heard, "Patrow. See Jeff."

Well, I strutted in there with my chest so puffed up I actually looked like I might wear a 36C. I was a little nervous but very proud of myself. *Somebody* thought I had talent. *Ha-ha.*

"What the hell is this?" he said, holding out my resignation.

So of course I said, "My resignation" (followed by a silent "na-na-na-na-na-na").

"You don't want to go to Champaign, for God's sake."

"They want me to be on the air."

"What are they paying you? It can't be what I'm paying you."

"It doesn't matter. (Actually, it did. I'd be taking a pay cut of about $10,000.) I want to be on the air."

"I'll give you a raise if you stay."

"I'll only stay if you'll let me voice scripts and be on the air."

"I'll only let you do that if you get voice lessons."

"I'll get voice lessons if you pay for them."

"Done."

I was so unprepared for that exchange that I wondered if it had really happened. But I got Jeff's promise in writing, along with a nice, fat raise.

I deserved it, considering he had made me feel so shitty.

But the deal here was that what I went through, what Jeff "did" to me, was the ultimate blessing. Had he not crushed my dream, I would not have gotten off my ass when I did and been so fierce about pursuing it just to spite him. Had he not demanded voice lessons, there was no way I would have gotten my dream reporting job in the Twin Cities. (My voice *was* pretty bad, I have to admit.)

Without Jeff crushing my dream, I wouldn't have fought so hard to realize it. He, unintentionally, was my dream's miracle.

"Olympic Trials"

Jill is an amazingly strong, talented woman. She is one of the best news photographers and directors I've ever known, and she has never let the "old boys' network" in news hold her back. She can go from making you shake in your boots (if you screw up one of her shoots), to making you chicken soup when you get sick. She's loyal to a fault and has been one of my best friends ever. That's why the fact that I almost screwed up a miracle for her makes me cringe. Fortunately, the miracle was hell-bent on happening anyway.

It was back in 1994. Jill and I were working at a production company in Chicago. She directed all of our shows, and I was a producer—which meant, according to Jill, that I had to do what she said. It was exciting work for someone young and single in Chicago, getting to travel all over the country, shooting videos and doing live satellite teleconferences. But it was all-consuming work and didn't allow for much of a life outside of work—unless you count Jill and I going out and drinking after work nearly every night, but since we're heterosexual, it wasn't entirely satisfying. We spent our non-drinking free time looking for other jobs that were more life-friendly and closer to our respective dreams: mine being a reporter in Minneapolis and hers being a director for the next Olympics in Atlanta.

Enter, yet another teleconference assignment. This time, I'd be producing a "two-fer"—two cities— Miami first, then up to Boston for the same thing the next day. I tried my damnedest to get out of it. Couldn't someone else go? No. How about just one city instead of two? After all, they'd be talking about the same shit, just from a different city. Still no. I bitched and complained the entire time, vowing not to enjoy any part of it. Jill totally empathized. As far as we were concerned, this whole production gig couldn't be over with fast enough.

So there I was for my umpteenth, brain-numbing, marathon assignment in the control room of this teleconference, reluctantly chatting it up with the crew from Boston. I kept ignoring a feeling that I should go talk to the floor director Lynn. But the feeling persisted. So finally, out of sheer boredom, I began talking to her. As we chatted, she mentioned that she had been looking at Atlanta for work but wasn't really that crazy about the city. And I said how I had a good friend who loved it and wanted to work for the Olympics there.

And then Lynn said she knew the people at the broadcasting company for the Olympics and would be happy to give me their names! So I took them down, and after the teleconference I called Jill's answering machine and laid the info on her. Could that have been why I got sent to Boston? She got my message and called the broadcasting company on Monday. The guy there couldn't believe that she'd called, because the woman they'd hired to do the job had just reneged on them for another offer, and they needed someone like Jill—*now*. She faxed a resume; they called back, interested as all get-out. She flew down a couple of days later and got hired *just like that*. It was meant to be. So much so, it's scary.

I wrote in my diary that night how elated I was that Jill was getting a shot at her dream … how sad I was that she would be going … how much I was going to miss her. I told God and Jesus they'd better take care of her. Then I realized, they just had.

"Layoff with a Payoff"

Not long after Dave and I left TV news, we were invited to a friend's wedding reception. It was great; we got to see a lot of friends we used to work with at the TV station. Many of them, like us, chose to leave after the new management came in. Some, like our friend Jill, had no choice. She was let go.

Jill had been the producer of the consumer-reports segment of the five o'clock news. She was really good at it, which was kind of funny if you knew Jill, because the nature of the segment was to expose seedy business practices, which of course pisses off a lot of people. Jill is a small, sweet-looking person with big, beautiful doe-eyes, and she rarely made a peep at work. I imagined she must have a Sybil-like side of her that sent creepy business owners running for cover.

Anyway, when I found out she'd been fired a few months earlier, I felt bad for her. She and her husband had just bought a house and were in the process of trying to adopt a child. Her job had provided their medical insurance as well. Jill hadn't seen it coming, but on March 11, 2005, she'd gone in to work, a full-time employee, and had come home without a job.

That's why I was so surprised when she hurried over and embraced me at the reception, just beaming. She told me that they had just gotten their "referral," which, in adoption language, meant they'd been assigned a baby—a little boy in Guatemala. He'd be "home" within a couple of months. She promised she'd bring her purse over and show me some pictures.

After dinner, a hand holding a glossy three-by-five picture appeared in front of my face. The picture was of beautiful baby Jackson; the hand belonged to Jill. There was that big smile again. So I got up to hug her. "No wonder you're so happy," I said.

"You know," she said, "I thought March 11th was the worst day of my life. Turns out, it was the best."

I asked her what she meant. She smiled.

Her new job had better hours and better pay; and even though she had just started it, they were giving her a full three-months' paid maternity leave for when Jackson came home. But that was nothing compared to the real miracle of that day, she said.

"Not only did I find a job that's better for us as a family," she said. "I also found out that the day I got fired … was the very day Jackson was born: March 11, 2005."

"The Pink Slip Present"

I was driving to work early one morning, which, in the dead of a Minnesota winter, still looks and feels like the dead of night. Seven a.m., and it's still pitch-black outside, blowing snow particles that make cars' headlights look like fuzzy searchlights scouring the highway. It was so cold I could see my breath *inside* the car.

Then the day got bad.

As I turned into the icy driveway at Channel 9, my little Toyota Celica began to skid down the slight downhill slope toward the parking area. Flashes of my high school drivers' ed classes had me pumping the brakes, steering in the direction of the skid, blah-blah-blah. I think they just tell you that stuff to make you feel like you're doing something in a situation you can really do nothing about because, despite my efforts, I slid right into the side of a parked car. A brand-new Lexus. The brand-new Lexus that belonged to one of the anchors of our show. Yeah, good times.

Deciding to take this job hadn't been easy. I had been at Channel 11, the number-one station in town; and for a while, it was great. I loved reporting. Then they wanted me to anchor their new early-morning show, which was flattering. But it meant getting up at 1:30 a.m., getting in to work by 3:00, and being on the air—looking like I loved it—at 5:00 a.m. *Then* … I might get to go out and report until 11:00 when my day was done. I agreed to give it a try for three months, provided that if I didn't like it, I could go back to reporting full-time.

I didn't like it. First: I hardly got to do any of my first love, reporting. Second: I had to go to bed by 6:30 p.m. to get any semblance of a night's sleep. And at age thirty and newly-divorced, that pretty much nixed any hopes of a social life. Let me rephrase that. Nixed any hopes of a *life*—period. Plus, my sleep deprivation left me feeling sick most of the time.

So after three months, I went into the news director's office as we had agreed and told him thank you so much for the opportunity, but I wanted my old job back. Oops. Too bad. He said that my old job didn't exist anymore and that it was this job or nothing. I had been too trusting, too naïve. Now I was stuck. And the pay sucked. I told him I'd have to think about it: a two-year contract for a hellish schedule and terrible pay, plus a one-year non-compete clause after that (i.e., you belong to us). So, after much deliberation and deep talks over beers with my friends, I went and got another job at Channel 9 across town, reporting for a new national show they were going to launch called NewScope.

They offered to pay $7,000 more a year as a reporter than I would have made as an anchor at Channel 11. And my hours would be 7:00 to 3:30, Monday through Friday. Not as prestigious, but at least I wouldn't wake up at age forty realizing that I had slept most of my life away.

But NewScope had its own problems. Initially, it was supposed to be this half-hour hard-news program covering world events, societal issues, and health news. (Health news was my specialty; I loved it.) But then for some reason they changed their minds and decided they wanted it to be more of a Regis and Kathie Lee (now Kelly Ripa)-type show, which none of us had any idea of how to do. They changed the name to "Everyday Living." Then they changed the "anchors" from serious news journalists to folksy, chatty busybodies who laughed a lot and made fun of each other's personal business. We "underlings" (reporters) were told we had to be wackier, more neighborly types who'd go out and try quirky things, then come back and show the audience our silly outtakes on tape, and finally show them "how to" do whatever it was that was wacky that week.

I was miserable. I hated wacky. I hated chatty. I hated "teaching" the audience how to do Tai Chi or make tofu when there were experts who could do it much better than I—assuming that anyone was really interested in making tofu in the first place. I wanted to be out in the field reporting on serious issues, not in the studio, yukking it up with the wacky host "Stephen" (and you had to pronounce it *Steff*-un), pretending I thought he was hilarious and incorrigible. I really thought he was annoying and immature.

I had also wisely used my great schedule and resulting free time to hook up with another idiot boyfriend, Jim. Dark and handsome, he was a clone of my first husband, i.e., it wasn't going to work this time, either. (Read more about Jim in my "divorce" story.) So, personally and professionally, I was in hell. Once again, I felt sick all the time and incessantly questioned my decision to leave Channel 11.

Well, exactly one year after failing to be a reputable news program or a successful Regis-and-Kathie-Lee clone, management called a meeting. I remember it was a Monday, and by that time I had resigned myself to numbly completing my four-year contract and saving money to make a pilgrimage to some part of the world where no one would know that I had done an entire taped segment in my bra, being analyzed by a bra expert, on the premise that 80 percent of American women were wearing the wrong size bra, which causes a variety of health problems. (I *was* wearing the wrong size, by the way). So I did learn a valuable lesson from it. But I was still on TV in my bra.

To my surprise, management didn't have any more crazy ideas. In fact, they had no ideas at all. They had decided to pull the plug. We were being cancelled and laid off ... in five days. Our last show would be that Friday. I remember the shocked silence in the room as all of us "wacky" folks stared blankly at each other.

I had never been laid off before. If you ever have, you know the feeling—like a puppet with no strings. Or that flailing, I-can't-swim feeling. I had no job prospects. I didn't even have a current resume. I'd just bought a townhouse. I had a dog to feed. And yet, I felt this overwhelming peace and relief. I kept waiting for the panic and tears to set in. People were crying all around me. But as we got nearer and nearer to Friday, I only got happier. At our "cancellation" party at a nearby Mexican restaurant, I remember my fellow unemployed and quickly intoxicated journalists asking me, "Aren't you sad? Aren't you scared?" And without thinking, I'd answer, "No. Everything's going to work out." And I totally believed it.

I remember going to bed that night and honestly trying to get myself all whipped up over what in the hell I was going to do. But all I kept hearing was, "It's all going to work out." So I said to God, "Hey, I don't know what's ahead; but this must be for the best, so just let me know what I'm supposed to do. And thanks." That night I slept better than I had in months.

Within two weeks I had an interview at the local ABC affiliate, Channel 5, for a freelance reporter position. They were embarking on a new approach to news, with new management and a new philosophy built on the highest ethical and moral standards. They had brought in the best news photojournalists in the business. Quality, responsible reporting was their goal. I felt like I had come home. Two days later they offered me the job and I took it.

Looking back, that layoff was the one of the best professional and personal experiences I ever had. The show I hated made me focus on what I loved about news, and I would settle for nothing less in my next job. At Channel 5, I was able to do the best reporting I ever did in my life: I won awards; I worked with the best journalists and photojournalists in the country; and I helped my station win the national Station of the Year award—twice. And I met and married the love of my life, Dave—one of the best photojournalists at the station.

Kind of like going through a divorce, going through a layoff can either leave you bitter and "poor-me"-ing yourself (which is such an attractive quality to bring into your next job interview). Or you can look at what that job taught you, how it made you a better—or at least wiser—person, and bless it for preparing you for what's next.

As for leaving Channel 11, I never again doubted my decision. It took that, and the year in purgatory at Channel 9, to get to my miracle job and my wonderful marriage. In 20/20 hindsight, it was perfect timing—not fast, by any means, but perfect, nonetheless. A miracle worth waiting for.

"Photo-Finished?"

One of the first things you learn in the news business is not to bury the lead. So here it is:

Jim Gehrz was named the "2005 Best of Photojournalism Newspaper Photographer of the Year."

I could end the story right there, because when you consider all of the newspapers in all of the cities and towns in this country and all the pictures they use every day, that's a miracle right there. *This* guy's pictures were voted the best. But the miracle's even more astonishing when you learn that, twenty-one years earlier, a director of photography at a major newspaper said these words to him:

"You do not have an eye for photographs. No matter how hard you work, you will *never* have an eye. So you might as well quit the photojournalism business and start painting houses."

Jim says those words are as clear in his memory today as the day he heard them. And he *could* have quit, taken the man's word for it, and taken up painting houses (which earns you a lot more money than taking pictures, by the way). But he didn't. And the ensuing journey from that point to this award was the biggest miracle of all—a miracle of timing, perseverance, and heart.

Jim was the youngest of six kids, born to academically-accomplished parents. His dad was a lawyer; his mom graduated from Northwestern University. Both earned Phi Beta Kappa status with their impressive grade point averages. His siblings were cut from the same cloth: they did great in school and had big aspirations in medicine and science. Then there was Jim. He did fine in school, but not great. He was a good kid, quiet and contemplative. His aspirations and gifts were not immediately clear. But he did seem to gravitate toward his older brother Bob (a future astrophysicist) whenever he disappeared into his darkroom downstairs to develop the pictures he had taken as a hobby. As Jim puts it, he loved the ability of pictures to freeze a moment in time and bring you back to that time in an instant.

When he was in sixth grade, Jim found out he was getting a Kodak Instamatic camera for Christmas. If you're as old as I am, you'll remember it was one of those small, box-like, black-and-white numbers with a big flash-cube on the top. You had to manually roll the film in order to take the next picture and change the flash-cube every four times you used it. And every time you did use it, someone in the picture turned out looking like Satan because of the red-eye effect it caused. But of course back then the Kodak Instamatic was the coolest.

Anyway, Jim was so excited at the prospect of having his own camera that, before Christmas, he carefully unwrapped the present, took the camera out, rewrapped the box, and put it under the tree. He says he took about twenty rolls of film on the sly before Christmas, then snuck it back in the box and rewrapped it again, just so he could open it Christmas morning.

To backtrack a little, Jim's mother died when he and his twin brother were eight, leaving Jim's father with the prospect of raising six kids on his own. But Jim's father held firm to his and his late wife's expectations of their children. Like when Jim's sister, Betty, told her dad that she was thinking about becoming a pharmacist and he persuaded her to consider medical school instead. She's now a physician, as is his brother, Dick. Two other brothers – Bill and Bob – became physicists; and his twin, Tom, is a carpenter.

Gradually the Gehrz children left the nest to pursue their educations and careers. But it was brother Bob's departure that hit Jim the hardest. When he moved out, he took all of his photography equipment and his darkroom with him. Jim's father could see that his youngest child was devastated.

While Jim's path in life continued to baffle his father, he did sense how important photography seemed to be to the boy. So one Saturday morning he said to Jim, "Let's go run an errand." When they pulled up in front of Fisher Photo in downtown St. Paul, Jim had no idea what to think. And he couldn't believe his ears when his dad told the saleswoman to gather whatever was needed for Jim to take pictures and develop them on his own.

Jim was beside himself. First of all, in the Gehrz household, you only got presents on your birthday and at Christmas. Second, Jim hadn't thought his dad understood his passion for photography. So on both fronts, Jim was elated. And soon it became clear that the youngest of the Gehrz family was gravitating toward a career in photography.

Jim did an internship at a small newspaper during college, then got a freelance job for another small paper called *The Highland Villager*. That was when photography first became a means of earning a living, if you could call it that. He and his wife and baby lived in a one-bedroom apartment in which their bathroom doubled as a darkroom. For six years he developed all of his pictures in there. He laughs as he remembers that when he tried sell a few of his pictures at a local art show, the only offer he got was for the easel they were displayed on. Then he got his big break.

The picture editor for the *St. Paul Pioneer Press* called one day and asked him to freelance. That's one of the two biggest newspapers in the state. Then, shortly after he started, a graphics director who had the reputation of being somewhat intense surprisingly took Jim aside (on Christmas Eve, no less) and told him he "saw something" in his work, that he was going to invest time in him. He gave him books to take home and study and then told him that if he worked really hard, he would consider him for a full-time job opening in the spring. Jim couldn't believe it. He couldn't wait to share the news with his wife and young son, because money had been tight, and this would mean a substantial boost in income. Finally, he would be able to get out of the bathroom to produce his pictures.

So he did exactly what the graphics director told him to do. He studied those books, and he worked really hard, pushing his abilities and finessing the fine points of his photography. So when that position came open in the spring, Jim assembled what he thought was a pretty good portfolio for the man to consider.

Well, Jim couldn't have been more wrong. Not about the portfolio, but about the man's consideration for his work. Jim describes the "interview" this way:

"We never even sat down. It was in an outer area of the dark room. I handed him the portfolio, and he took it and just ripped the pages out and threw them all over the floor. He didn't even look at my pictures. It was very cruel. And while I'm there on the floor, picking my pictures up, he's explaining, "These are terrible! These are so bad …""

He didn't stop there. With Jim scrambling about on his knees, desperately trying to salvage his portfolio, that's when the director of photography said those terrible words:

"You do not have an eye for photographs. No matter how hard you work, you will never have an eye. So you might as well quit the photojournalism business and start painting houses."

Jim was dumbstruck. Not because he thought his photographs were the best; in fact, he knew that there were more seasoned photographers vying for the same job. But he thought he'd at least get fair consideration. In the dimly lit lobby area outside the darkroom, Jim realized that this man was trying to do more than deny him a job. He was trying to crush his spirit.

And the man succeeded—for a little while. Jim said he was crying as he drove home that day to deliver the bad news to his family. But the more he thought about it, the more he realized that this was a turning point in his career, if not in his life.

"It made me realize that no matter where you are in your personal journey as a photojournalist, no one ever has the right to crush your spirit. People certainly have the right to express that they feel you are not ready for a certain job or that your style is not what they are looking for. But everyone who feels the calling to be a visual journalist has the right—even a duty—to pursue that dream."

Ever since Jim had been a kid, he'd felt the calling to be a photojournalist; and he couldn't believe he'd been wrong all that time. So he filed the man's comments in his that's-only-one-person's-opinion file and worked even harder. About a month after this ordeal, Jim worked tirelessly to put together an entry for the weekly newspaper state photographer of the year—and won. He said it was his way of not letting that man's opinion be the last word on his work. From *The Highland Villager* to Worthington to Milwaukee, Jim's photos captured the best and the hardest moments of people's lives. His greatest satisfaction came from producing photos that, as he calls it, "communicated hope" in some way; hope that the world still has good in it, and hope in the resiliency of the human spirit.

Like his own.

Year after year, he kept improving, kept entering contests for news photography and winning. And year after year, he kept applying to the major Twin Cities newspapers: the *Minneapolis Star Tribune* four times and the *St. Paul Pioneer Press* eight times. He never got the job, but he never quit trying.

Jim was working in Milwaukee when his dad got sick. Lung cancer. Jim needed to come home. Magically, both the *Star Tribune* and the *Pioneer Press* had openings just then, although by this point, Jim admits, he didn't much care anymore. But he needed to be near his dad. So, once again, he submitted his portfolio to both.

And this time, they noticed. On the same day, within an hour of each other, both papers called and asked him to come in for interviews. And it was the Pioneer Press – the very paper where the graphics director nearly crushed Jim's dream more than twenty years before – that promptly offered him a job: *the* job that would allow him to come home exactly when he needed to and make the kind of living he needed to make.

A week after he started his new job, his father died. But it was during that week that Jim says he got to know his father better than he ever had. The old Navy WWII vet had been the strong, silent type all his life, but the prospect of death allowed him to open up. Jim learned that he was very much like his dad after all—a man who, when confronted with adversity like the untimely death of Jim's mother, channeled that energy and grief into working harder and not letting it define his life.

Jim also credits his dad with honing his own definition of success. In the end, his dad refused any last-ditch medical treatments that might keep him alive for a short time longer. He chose to come home and have his kids around him. He chose family and quality of life over some doctors' opinions of what he *should* do. Jim too has gauged his success by keeping his family his priority, and photojournalism his passion. His definition of success is not ambition, defined by the news business as traveling the world and putting yourself in harm's way to deliver the story. Rather, he defines success as reaching his own potential close to home, where his heart is, and taking pictures that are more Norman Rockwell than sensational point-and-shoot snapshots.

So, really, it's a 20/20-hindsight kind of miracle for Jim. Looking back, he views his earlier run-in with that graphics director as his own personal miracle: one that gave him resolve for his life's work; one that sent him on a journey to improve his craft in a way that small papers can do; and one that allowed him—called him, even—to come home right when he needed it most, to be with and get to know his father.

And after nearly four years at the *Pioneer Press*, Jim took a full-time job at the *Star Tribune,* where he remains today, and where he wound up winning Best Photographer of the Year.

How to See Miracles in Your Own Job—or Lack of One

For some expertise in seeing "job miracles," I consulted Gaye Lindfors, a strategic business advisor who specializes in helping business leaders build organizations where people want to do their best work every day. During her twenty-five years in leadership positions with Fortune 500 companies and nonprofit organizations, Gaye observed that the companies with high-performing cultures had one thing in common: employees who felt a sense of significance at work and in life. Using this insight, Gaye developed her human-centered (and more miracle-oriented) approach to business success called "Significant Solutions." Here's what Gaye has to say about how to see your job or lack of one in a more miraculous light.

Even a not-so-good work experience has its gifts. It can give you clarity about what you don't want to do or who you don't want to work for. Keep track of those lessons learned and use them for your next job search. It's information you wouldn't have known had you not gone through that tough experience.

If you've got difficult coworkers, remember that their lives are bigger than their job titles. Maybe something is going on in their personal lives that's negatively impacting how they behave at work—and toward you. *Show mercy,* and be someone else's miracle. Watch for—or create—the opportunity to make a colleague's day better. Think about what your colleague will say about you at the dinner table tonight. What do you want them to say?

Losing your job can be frustrating and scary. Allow yourself those emotions. But realize that it also offers a gift that most employed people long for: time to enjoy the things you really care about, like travel, family, or hobbies. So during this time of transition, manage your daily schedule wisely; take the time to visit that museum or see that friend or write that first novel. Treat it as the vacation you never allowed yourself while you were employed.

The most important thing to remember, Gaye says, is that no matter what happens, you will always have the title of "Manager of My Career." Don't delegate that to anybody. Typically we wait for someone to notice us or promote us or tell us what we need to do to get to the next level. No, that's *your* job. And owning that responsibility puts you in charge of creating your own job miracles.

My husband Dave—who has been laid off twice—also has a great perspective on this whole job-miracles thing. He says if you really think about it, pretty much every business and job exists to provide or do something "good." No matter what you do, you provide a service. You produce something people need. You contribute ideas to make life better in some way. Big picture? We're all working on some level to help each other. Isn't that a miracle?

Keep track of your little victories, even if nobody else notices. You met a deadline. You helped a coworker. You came up with a better idea for getting something done. These are your contributions—your daily miracles—to the world. See yourself as a "miracle-maker," and any job you have feels worthwhile.

We're all bound to have "those days" on the job (or while we're looking for one) when nothing seems to go right. On such days, just remember what you're working for: your spouse, your children, and your home. Remembering the real miracles in your life will give you the incentive to keep going and do your job (or your job search) well.

Chapter Four: Money Miracles

Being in News Gave Me a Whole Different Perspective on Money.

First, as a reporter, you rarely have any, and you quickly realize that for most of your career you'll never have a lot of it. So you've got to let that go. Second, the more you report, the more you realize that money—whether it's the lack of it or the greed for more of it—can cause people to do bad things.

After reporting on so many Ponzi schemes, gas station holdups, church break-ins, and divorce settlements, I don't respect money as an end in itself. I see it more as a means to living the life you desire. I know; it's a small nuance. But focus on life rather than the money, and oftentimes the money or the means to get it shows up in ways you never expected.

"Liquid Assets"

It was hard to convince me to have another garage sale. My first one had been chaotic. I hadn't been exposed to that unique breed of bargain shoppers before: rifling through my stuff; bickering with each other as to who saw what first; trying to talk me down in price from one-dollar to fifty cents—for a brand new CD. I mean, come on.

One lady was so frantic about hoarding her purchases in her van that she left a pile of purchased stuff behind. Never came back for it either. I don't think she even knew what she'd bought—only that it was cheap.

But this time another couple, Mike and Jen, agreed to have the sale with us. They'd bring their stuff over, help price it, and sit with us all day to sell it. So I thought, why not? My husband and I had just moved into our house and needed to get rid of our single-life stuff.

That Sunday was sunny and warm. We had a steady stream of people in the morning who were much more pleasant than I expected. My CDs sold for a dollar (no bickering), and there was no frantic pawing at items between customers. By afternoon, my living room set and Mike and Jen's tables and lamps were about the only "must-sell" items left. We had them nicely arranged in the driveway, like a living room with no roof, but our river of customers dwindled to a trickle. 3:00. 4:00. Our sale was only until 6:00. We began pondering the possibility of having to haul all that furniture back into our respective basements, then out again to a consignment shop or Goodwill. Not good. Then at 5:30 a Jeep pulled up.

A sweaty but happy-looking mom got out, her sandals flip-flopping as she walked around and opened the passenger door for her daughter. Their jeep was packed to the hilt with what looked like the contents from fourteen garage sales: lawn chairs, coolers, balls, lamps, clothing, etc.

She introduced herself as Sandy; her daughter Theresa was nine. She laughingly said they were on their way back to Wisconsin after visiting her older daughter who worked at Regis Corporation (where Jen worked) and had gotten lost. They were driving around and saw our garage sale, so they thought they'd stop for some bargains and directions.

Where in Wisconsin were they from? I asked. Chippewa Falls—my home town! Come to find out that she was the daughter of a retired judge in town whom my mom knew. Sandy had just gotten divorced and was moving into her dad's big, old house—known throughout town as the old judge's house—and needed to furnish it.

Was this furniture all for sale? she asked, marveling. Oh, yes, we said. (We had been about to offer to pay someone to take it away, but we didn't tell her that.)

Theresa played with our dog Max as Sandy walked around the set, imagining it this way and that in her father's house. We'll take it, she said. All of it. Only, could we hold on to it until she could drive over with a trailer?

It was 5:55 p.m. In one fell swoop, a cheese-head from my own hometown had taken a wrong turn and inadvertently come to our rescue. She claimed that we had come to hers. She wrote out a check and was gone.

All told, Mike and Jen made about $350; Dave and I made $470. But that's not the end of this story. After packing it all in from our garage sale, we went downstairs into the family room, only to find the carpet soaking wet. One of our pipes had burst. Dave did his best to slow the leak, but it definitely could not wait till morning. We had to call an emergency plumber—on a Sunday night, after 5:00 p.m. (Translation: big bucks.)

Our bill for that? $465. Really. Go figure.

"Glad Tithings"

My friend Chris is a very strict Catholic. She knows the Bible inside and out; recites the rosary as naturally as breathing; and regularly goes to confession (even though she has nothing to confess, at least compared to people like me). She even stayed a virgin until she got married … at age thirty-six.

Now, Chris's view of religion would never allow her to believe she is worthy of a miracle, but it was one of her religious practices that brought her one anyway. She was in her early twenties and living in England. Even though she was basically living paycheck to paycheck, she still managed to give ten percent of her income to the church. But then it got cold, and a heating bill entered the mix. She needed that eighty-eight dollars to pay the landlord for heat, or she'd be out of her apartment altogether. She worked it over and over in her head, how she could pay both the church and her rent that month. There was no way. Chris being Chris, she dug out her old winter coat, bundled up, and went to church to pray about it.

Chris says at the time she didn't get any clear answers or even intuitions about what to do. She prayed, sat quietly, and prayed some more. She finally decided that the guilt of not giving the church her money would burden her more than wrangling with the landlord about money, so she took the eighty-eight dollars out of her purse right then and there and put it in the tithing box.

She gave one last listen for an answer as she bundled up again to head into the cold. Nothing. She tucked her chin down and stuck her hands in her pockets to brave the cold—and felt something. Something, wedged way down in the bottom of the pocket that she hadn't had her hand in since last winter. She pulled it out. It was a small pack of bills folded over once and flattened by the weight of being packed away for winter. She began to count. Eighty-eight dollars. She counted again, her heart pounding. Eighty-eight dollars. Chris glanced around. No trumpets blaring. No angels singing. It was just her, alone in church. She never again questioned whether she'd have enough money.

"Serious Misgivings"

If you don't think miracles can happen at grocery stores, check *this* out!

My husband Dave and I had just come back from my birthday weekend at a bed and breakfast. We had opted to sleep in rather than take showers that morning, so we were looking a little grungy and road-weary in our T-shirts and jeans. When we walked in the door, Dave went straight to the phone to call his son Ryan, so we could arrange to pick him up from his mom's house. Well, the phone was dead. No dial tone. Nothing.

To make matters worse, my cell phone battery was out of juice. No neighbors were home. So we hopped back in the car and drove to Cub Foods, our nearby grocery store, to use the pay phone.

I immediately got on one phone to AT&T about our dead phone, while Dave searched his pockets for change to call Ryan on the other phone. He didn't have any. And I had used my last quarter to call AT&T. Meanwhile, I'd found out that they cut our phone service because I "didn't pay my phone bills." *What* phone bills? I asked. The three they'd sent—*to the wrong address*! I couldn't believe it. Well, they said they could reconnect me if I could give them the three hundred dollars I owed. I didn't have three hundred dollars! Dave and I had just gotten married a couple of months before. Few newly married couples I know have three hundred dollars to throw at a phone company in one chunk.

Not only did I not have the three hundred dollars to give the phone company; I didn't have any change to give Dave to call Ryan. Meanwhile, a gentleman was waiting to use the phone. So Dave apologetically stepped aside as I argued my case to the phone company. Dave motioned that he was going to go get change for a dollar bill. I nodded.

By the time Dave got back, the gentleman who'd replaced him at the pay phone was finishing his phone call. I didn't pay much attention, until I saw Dave hurrying after the man, waving his hand frantically and calling after him. But the man kept going, waving Dave off. He never looked back.

Dave did. At me. With eyes wide open and shock forcing his mouth into a disbelieving "O." And it wasn't because I had masterfully convinced the phone company to turn our phone back on. No, this was something even more impressive than that. I could see it in his eyes.

Dave held out his hand, and uncurled his fist. In it lay a crumpled hundred-dollar bill. I looked at Dave, confused. He said the man had given it to him and simply said: "For your trouble."

Looking back, I can see how the circus of phone calls we were making and the clothes we were wearing made us look, well, a little destitute. It occurred to me that the man had overheard me pleading my case as a young newlywed to the phone company and telling them we didn't have the three hundred dollars they wanted to turn our phone back on. He had seen Dave digging for change and asking me for some, which I didn't have any either. He had waited patiently, watching us try to do our family business on pay phones.

He had cared.

The funny thing is, this man didn't look like the kind of guy who had a hundred dollars to spare. He looked so "average" that neither Dave nor I can really remember what he looked like or what he was wearing. I just remember the silhouette of him quickly walking away and disappearing into the store parking lot.

I wished I could have thanked that man. Dave and I felt embarrassed—we didn't *need* the hundred dollars. Not like that. So we didn't spend it. Instead, I kept it in a special envelope and carried it with me for over a year, waiting for our turn to pass it on to someone who *really* needed it. That someone showed up the next spring.

Out of the blue, one of my coworkers asked me if I would do a favor for a friend of his. His friend was the principal of an elementary school, and the school was holding a fundraiser for a little Hmong boy who had cancer. His family didn't have insurance. Would I be so kind as to help host this event, since my coworker had other commitments?

It was a sweet, disorganized gathering, with a potluck hodge-podge of foods oozing over several card tables pushed together. Moms and dads and kids stood in line to tie bracelets of yarn around the little boy's wrist: a Hmong tradition for wishing someone well. The boy's father shyly thanked the crowd in broken English. The little boy beamed as he fidgeted in his traditional Hmong outfit, complete with jangly copper pieces hanging off his sleeves. He was a joy to behold. At the end, his classmates filed up to the front of the gym and sang songs for him.

Dave and Ryan had come to see me host the event. The last part of it was a silent auction. The three of us perused the collection of items, not really intending to buy anything. And just before the bidding was over, I came upon three Van Gogh prints that I thought would go nicely in our home. There were several bids: the highest, ninety dollars. I thought, what the heck. I bid one hundred dollars and left it at that.

Three days later, the school called. We had "won" the Van Goghs with our bid of one hundred dollars. That hundred dollars would go directly to help the little boy with cancer. I took it as *the sign*. I gave Dave the hundred-dollar bill the man at the grocery store had given us so long ago. It had to be *that* hundred dollars, I knew. So Dave dropped by the school on his way to work and gave them the money in exchange for the prints.

I wish I could tell the man in Cub Foods that his money did help someone who really needed it. I wish he could see the smile on that little boy's face. When I think of the whole chain of events, maybe Dave and I were just the link the Cub Foods Angel needed to reach that little boy. Maybe he couldn't get there himself. If that's the case, I'm honored he chose us. He not only reminded us that there are good people in the world. Carrying around that hundred-dollar bill for as long as we did made us look for—and *see*—true need. It made us appreciate what we had. For a year, his hundred-dollar bill taught us important lessons about gratitude and giving. And when it was time, we bestowed his gift on the one who really needed it.

He gave the gift of gratitude to us, and the gift of life to that little boy.

"The Wealth Benefits of Yoga"

One of the great misperceptions about people who work in television news is that we make a lot of money. It's more accurate to think of us as a bunch of stressed-out monks (except for that vow of celibacy). My first job as a reporter paid a whopping $11,700 a year—which was fine as long as I was single and happy to live in a dump and eat pizza every day.

That's when I met my best friend, Sharon. She was a reporter at the same station and just as poor. She had just ruined her only pair of "good shoes"—Nine West pumps that she had saved for—by walking through a farm field doing a story on corn prices. One of the first lessons you learn as a reporter is to buy your shoes at Payless.

Fast-forward twenty years. We'd both gotten out of "the biz," but somehow that vow of poverty seemed to follow us around from time to time. By then Sharon had a husband, a stepson, twin girls, two big dogs, two car payments, and a cat—all of which had driven her to take up yoga when she could afford it. But it was an indulgence that she found hard to reconcile when the car broke down or one of the dogs got a rash and needed to go to the vet.

One night, she went to a yoga open house to try out some free classes (and free food). She was really drawn to the Jivamukti Yoga. (I don't know what that means, but she says it's the ultimate in relaxation and meditation.) Unfortunately, it was $125 for an eight-week series, no small amount of money when there are four other people, two dogs, and a cat to consider.

Which all added up to why she really *needed* yoga in the first place. How could she make it work? She took out her checkbook and scanned the register, hoping to find another "indulgence" she could do without so she could take the classes. She was leaning on the front desk, hoping against hope that the check she was writing wouldn't bounce, when the Yogi in charge saw Sharon's name on her checks. "Wait! Wait!" she said. "You've won!"

It turned out that when Sharon had arrived at the open house, she'd put her name in for a prize drawing. She hadn't heard it when they called her name, but she had won $95 toward the class of her choice. So, what would have cost her $125 was now only going to cost $30. *That* she could afford.

The lady handed the check back to Sharon and smiled. "It must be karma." (This is a very yoga thing to say.)

"Must be," Sharon told her.

I asked Sharon what went through her mind at that very moment. Here's what she wrote:

"You know what went through my mind? I have to tell you, stuff like this has happened my whole life. It used to drive Kevin (her old boyfriend) crazy. I'd be down to my last ten dollars, and I'd get some refund check from State Farm. Or after my U-Haul was broken into in Chicago, the Bank of Tokyo told me I had left a two-hundred-dollar balance in my checking account. I told them I had cleared my account, but they wouldn't believe me and sent the money anyway. I went and bought stereo speakers, since I had a stereo but no speakers, no radio, and no TV. Of course, six months later they did an audit and—oops! The money wasn't mine, but it was a timely loan!

I don't know; maybe it *is* good karma!

"That's Entertainment"

After three years of marriage, Dave and I finally decided to buy a new TV and a stand for our family room. The one we had was pretty old, from my pre-Dave days, and the entertainment center it sat in was from my previous marriage. Yup. Time to let go.

When our new TV arrived, we put the old one in the laundry room. Surely some family member or friend would want it. But phone call after phone call turned up appreciative no-thank-yous. Either they already had enough TVs, or they wanted one of the newer, plasma varieties, not an old tube style.

So it sat there. For months. We tried the newspaper classifieds. Turns out the TV was worth less than what it cost to advertise it. So that took eBay out of the running too. But it was too good to just throw away. So we continued to sidle around it as we did our laundry day in and day out.

Finally one day after sucking in his gut to get by the thing for the hundredth time, Dave had had it. "We've got to do something with that TV!" I agreed. What about Goodwill or the Salvation Army? We called. One didn't take TVs or entertainment centers at all. The other would take the entertainment center but not the TV. I was looking through the Yellow Pages for county disposal sites when there was a knock on the door.

Dave opened it to find a middle-aged man in a T-shirt and jeans. He was holding pamphlets from the church he belonged to. He told us how he had been a drug addict, and how the church and Jesus Christ had helped turn his life around. Would we care to donate some money to the church? Dave asked him to wait a minute, got some money, and accepted a pamphlet in return. The man thanked him profusely and left.

Dave began to read the pamphlet and half-kiddingly said, "I wonder if *they'd* want the TV and entertainment center?" There was a phone number on the pamphlet, so we decided, what the heck?

The man who answered sounded so excited that he about jumped through the phone and got the TV himself. Yes, yes, they would love the TV and stand, and in fact, the minister of the church might still be in our neighborhood. He'd call his cell phone right away.

Sure enough. The minister called us immediately, saying he was just a couple of blocks away. And could we wait until he could pull his van around and come get it? We couldn't believe it.

In five minutes the man who had originally come to our door—and his minister—showed up in a beat-up, old church van. They wouldn't let Dave or me lift a finger. Gingerly they carried everything upstairs and into their van, thanking us all the way. They said how nice it would be for the men to have a TV to watch in the church recreation room; that they had not been able to afford one themselves. And how did we know it was exactly what they needed? It was a lesson in patience and appreciation. That, truly, is the ultimate entertainment.

"Taking the Heat"

My good friend Mellissa describes her mom "Carol" as a strong woman of great faith, with no qualms about listening for and acting on what she believes are messages from God, no matter what anybody thinks. One of those times was when Mellissa was in junior high.

Mellissa was "dating" a boy in her class. She uses the quotation marks because, in junior high, dating consisted of her parents or her boyfriend's parents driving and accompanying them on every so-called "date."

That's how Mellissa's mom got to know the boyfriend's mom and how she found out when the woman's husband just up and left them one day, with all the bills and no money to pay them. Back in those days, there wasn't any state assistance plan that kicked in if you couldn't pay your bills. So the family was facing a Wisconsin winter with no heat in their home.

That's when Carol got a "message" that she should pay that woman's heating bill, even though her own family was living paycheck to paycheck and couldn't really afford it. Carol kept listening. How much? she wondered. She came up with a figure in her head, and the message came back: "No, that's too little." So she thought again and the message came back: "No, that's too much." Soon a figure appeared in her mind that she knew was just right. So after work that day, she went home and wrote out a check to the woman and took it over to her house.

"Here," she said as the woman opened the door. "Here's money for your heating bill." The woman was overcome to begin with. But when she looked down at the check in her hands, her eyes widened in disbelief. "How did you know?" she said. "This is the exact amount of money I owe on my bill. Let me show you …" She offered to go get the bill, but Mellissa's mom waved her off. She already knew it was the right amount of money.

As far as making ends meet for her own family that month, Mellissa only remembers that her mom willingly "took the heat" from whomever criticized her for giving away money that they didn't have. She was confident that someway, somehow, everything would work out, and it did. Mellissa says she doesn't remember going without anything they needed, especially her mother's nice, "warm" smile.

"Dyer Circumstances"

I am a big fan of Dr. Wayne Dyer, the best-selling author and internationally renowned expert in the field of self-development. He teaches the concept of intention as a field of energy that each of us can use to co-create our lives, and he makes very compelling arguments for the power of intention, deliberate thought, and the spoken word to create our reality. I came upon his books when Dave and I both had been laid off from our jobs. (Note to self: it's best not to work for the same company when you're married; downsizing doesn't take into account whether your entire way of life depends upon one employer.) We had three kids, a mortgage, and two car payments to take care of, so this was an especially scary time. We viewed each mail delivery with fear as we busily sent out resume after resume, to no avail. I definitely needed to believe that things would get better, especially in the money department. So I decided to take Dr. Dyer up on some of his recommendations.

In *The Power of Intention*, Dr. Dyer teaches ways to visualize, articulate, and believe in the reality you desire to experience. It is important not to focus on what you lack, because that creates more lack, but rather to focus on abundance and the belief that you already have and will continue to have what you need. In my case, that was money. Bills were coming in, but money was not.

So I visualized paying my bills with confidence. I visualized full cupboards, full gas tanks, and a full bank account. I visualized being comfortable in our home and buying what we needed to get by. Then I said it out loud: "I desire A, B, and C. I see A, B, and C happening. I *have* A, B, and C." I repeated this over and over for days and then weeks, figuring that even if it didn't help, it wouldn't hurt.

The bills kept coming, to the point where I couldn't ignore them any longer no matter how much my positive intentions reassured me that abundance was on the way. Resigned, I sat down to go through the pile of mail I had blindly allowed to accumulate on our desk. This one, pay now. That one—we've got some time. This one, maybe, if I call … then, *wait*. In my hand was what I initially thought was a bill from our auto insurance company. But this time the envelope said, "Open Immediately. Do Not Discard." So I opened it. Inside was a check for over $300, our customer dividend from the company's successful year. I couldn't believe it. I looked at the postmark. It was three weeks old, so I'd had it for a while. In fact, it had arrived just about the time I'd started this whole intention-exercise thing. In that moment I got those chills you get when you suddenly feel a part of something bigger than yourself.

Now, you could write this off to coincidence rather than an act of creation. Maybe the fact that I was paying more attention to our finances through these exercises simply made me recognize something that was already there. Or maybe, just maybe, it was a miracle that showed up exactly when we needed it. I choose to believe—and continue to visualize, speak, and believe in—the latter.

"How to Have Faith in (and Create) Your Own Money Miracles"

As I said earlier, I don't have much respect for money as an end in itself. Besides, focusing on money requires math, and let me just say there's a reason I was an English major in college. So, other than the stories I've shared, I'm really in no position to offer money advice. Oddly enough, though, it was my English professor in college who shared a piece of advice that I've found handy when money issues (and many other kinds of issues) required my attention.

Professor Peter Fritzell, or "Fritz" as those of us mentored by him during his decades at Lawrence University call him to this day, must have been the original model for "Liberal Arts Professor" catalog: khaki pants, tweed jacket with patches on the elbows, and chronically wrinkled button-down shirt. His salt-and-pepper hair shagged over wire-rimmed glasses and cascaded into a beard he was in the habit of stroking when something amused him, which was often. His pant cuffs always were at war with some version of waterproof, thick-tread boot, like he'd just emerged from the duck blind. His classes were entertaining and brilliant, alternately shattering your view of the world and then reconstructing it in ways that made you feel like you'd just been let in on a big secret. After one class, which was one of the hardest and most humbling I'd ever taken, I asked him to be my adviser for the rest of my college career. To this day I consider it one of the best decisions I've ever made.

Fritz had many stories that started out innocently enough but wound up requiring you to take an honest (and often unflattering) look at yourself and admit you weren't quite as smart as you thought you were. One of my least favorite at the time—and most memorable ever since—was the story about the "key."

Fritz had us "follow" him on a verbal journey along a path—a wooded path, I think. Considering that Fritz was an avid hunter, I'm pretty sure he was leading us through some Upper Midwest forest or marsh where his boots competed only with his blaze-orange or camouflage outerwear. Anyway, off we went, trying to find our way "out." He had us "notice" this-and-that along the way, asking us what it might mean and how we would react. One of those things was a key that lay in our path. There was no indication of what or whom it belonged to; it was just a key. He asked each of us what we would do.

Like most of my classmates, I said I'd pick it up and put it in my pocket. Good enough, he said. Off we went again, as he pointed out other sights and sounds for clues on how to get out of the forest. I remember feeling a little impatient as we finally came upon some old, boarded-up building. By this point, I either wanted to learn something or get out of the damned forest. But Fritz went on to describe the unremarkable particulars of the abandoned schoolhouse, church, cabin, or whatever it was. He said we would try the door, only to find it locked. With no lights on inside and no signs of life, he said, what would we do? I can't remember what my classmates said, but I told him I'd stop wasting my time and keep walking.

I had forgotten. I had forgotten about the key in my pocket: the key, it turned out, not only to the door of that stupid building, but to getting out of the forest altogether. It was the key to getting "un-lost." Fritz's lesson was that I'd had the means to get out of the forest all along. I simply needed to remember the tools I carried with me.

For the last twenty-five years, that story has stayed with me. Whenever I'm "lost"—financially, emotionally, professionally, or personally—I stop and pay attention either to the tools I already have or to the "key in the path" that I happen upon along the way. It never fails. Something always shows up to help me find my way. So if you need a money miracle (and who doesn't at one time or another?) pay attention to the mail, to conversations, to opportunities for careers or classes that can increase your earning potential. I'm talking credentialed, valid opportunities here, not earn-a-million-bucks-in-a-year-type promises. (Remember, if it sounds too good to be true, it still is.) Just pay attention and look for your own key that could open the door to exactly what you need.

Chapter Five: Relationship Miracles

Whoever Came Up with the Phrase "Happily Ever After" Was Evil.

I mean, what other phrase has raised and then dashed so many hopes and dreams? What other phrase has put such high expectations on relationship skills for which none of us receives any training? We're all just fumbling around, trying to figure out how to play nicely in the same sandbox with each other without getting on anyone's nerves.

So, for those of us (all of us?) who have ventured and failed to achieve happily-ever-after—be it with boyfriends, girlfriends, siblings, parents, or friends—here is a bit of redemption. It's a way to look at your failures with compassion, appreciation, and an eye for the miracles that relationships give us along the way, helping us at least to achieve "happi*er*" ever after.

"Till Divorce Do Us Part"

Bear with me on this one. It's a long way to get to the miracle part, but I think about 50 percent of Americans could benefit from this experience, if current divorce rates are right.

My first marriage was to a tall, dark, handsome man named Bill—kind of Richard Gere-like but even better-looking. *Yum.* He was my college sweetheart. It made perfect sense. After all, I was a cute little cheerleader, and he was a star football player. Deep, right?

With that in common (and not much else) we got married in 1989. I have to confess that before my Dad walked me down the aisle, that little voice inside of me said, "Don't do it!" But I was a people-pleaser back then, and everybody said how we were meant to be together. Plus, I had this great dress. So I told the little voice to shut up, put on my best cheerleader smile, and marched confidently down the aisle to my football player.

It was a great wedding and honeymoon, I have to admit. The reception was a big, fun party with all of our friends. And the honeymoon was a surprise trip to Bermuda, courtesy of Bill's boss. But when all was said and done, and all the festivities were over, and we were alone living in Chicago, *marriage* set in.

Marriage is hard enough for couples who have a lot in common. So Bill and I were at a distinct disadvantage. I hated big cities. Bill loved Chicago and wanted to stay there forever. I wanted to be a TV news reporter, which I couldn't just up and do in Chicago with no experience. Bill wanted me to be his trophy wife: silent, smiling, and satisfied to be on his arm out in public. I was insecure about my abilities, just fresh out of college; Bill couldn't understand that and tried to humor me out of it by making fun of my demons. That only made me feel worse.

I was spiritual and believed in miracles and wasn't shy about celebrating them. I even skipped in public when my friend Jill and I got great seats for a Garth Brooks concert. Bill was either an atheist or agnostic, depending on the day. And when I skipped in public, he grabbed me by the elbow and told me to stop it because people would *see* me. Oh, the *embarrassment* of it all!

Now, I'm not saying that it's Bill's fault that we got divorced. I had pretended to be what he wanted (the people-pleaser thing again), and I could have been more giving and considerate of his needs too. And we were both young, thinking we were in love and doing the right thing. But as my life in Chicago and my marriage to him became more and more *not* me, I became more and more unhappy.

After almost four years of fighting and therapy, we got divorced.

You'd think that I'd have learned the big lesson about what I needed from a relationship. About what was important. Well, that would have been nice, I tell ya. But I was determined to date Bill-clones at least a couple more times before I got it.

There was "Pete" (his name changed here for his family's sake, not his), who looked a helluva lot like Bill: tall, dark, and strikingly handsome—the strong, silent type. We had what I thought was a great first date that ended with the appropriate level of making out at the end.

He never called again. Dumbfounded, I finally called him and said, "What's the deal?" He said it was because I sent him home with "blue balls" because I wouldn't have sex with him. Really. He was thirty-something years old and said "blue balls." I said, "I haven't heard *that* since high school! And besides, Pete, I don't sleep around." And he said, and I kid you not, "Yeah, what are ya? *Frigid?*" I couldn't believe it.

Still, I wasn't convinced that the tall, dark, handsome, shallow type wasn't for me. Enter, Jim—not so tall, but definitely dark (he went to a tanning booth religiously) and handsome. He slathered me with charm and presents right off the bat. I was bowled over. He even sent a gift basket of Milk Bones to my dog Max. I couldn't understand why Max never liked him. Hmm. First hint …

Anyway, once Jim had me hooked, he began the "isolating" thing. He didn't want me to talk to or spend time with Sharon or any other friends; he refused to socialize with my friends at parties; and he sulked when I forced him to join my family for a dinner out. If I wasn't with him, I wasn't supposed to be out. No matter that he spent more time with his golf and drinking buddies than he did with me. Then he'd act all defensive when I wanted some time with him, saying I was too demanding.

I thought I was losing my mind when a vacation we had planned together didn't materialize. We had confirmed the dates; I had taken time off of work. We were going to fly somewhere and spend an entire week together—to get me off his back, I presume. But as it got closer and closer to the date and "we" hadn't made any reservations, I began to get nervous. Jim kept saying, "Don't worry about it. I'll take care of it." Then that would be the last I'd hear about it, until I brought it up again. It was about a week before our vacation when I finally did, and he exploded, saying, well, he didn't think he could do it after all, that maybe he'd have to work, blah, blah, blah. It was the third or fourth time he'd broken this kind of promise (one time was my birthday). I lost it, and we had a big fight.

In tears, I called my mom (the kind of call she was getting used to), and she finally said, "Kris, if he really loved you, he wouldn't be doing this." I remember *hearing* that and subsequently making my own plane reservations for a vacation out to Seattle to see my good friend Lori. But I hadn't *listened* well enough not to get back with Jim one more time, just to make sure I couldn't make the good-looking guy into a good guy.

I couldn't.

Once Jim had charmed me back (and I let him), he started the same old neglect pattern—one that I later learned, had I married him, would likely have turned into abuse (isolation, chipping away at self-esteem, anger outbursts, etc.). This time my best friend Sharon stepped in. On a day that I called her from work in tears, she sent me an e-mail that read something like this:

> Hey, honey,
>
> This is hard for me to write, and it's going to be very hard for you to read, but I love you so much, and I don't want you to keep getting hurt like you are. So please forgive me if this makes you mad, but here goes.
>
> Bill and Pete and Jim are all the same guy: they're strikingly good-looking and successful, but they have no consistency, no substance. Yes, they look good on the outside. But they're kind of like filet-mignon. They're very "expensive" to have, and very rarely are they cooked just right or totally satisfying.
>
> What you need is more like a McDonald's "Happy Meal." You know, maybe they're not as fancy on the outside. But you know that once you get inside, it's *always* going to be good. No matter what day it is, or where you are, your Happy Meal is always going to make you happy.
>
> Please, honey. Go find your Happy Meal. You deserve it. I love you! Sharon

I remember reading that over and over again, feeling like Helen Keller must have felt once she understood how to spell *water*. For some reason, Sharon's words were what I needed, right when I needed them. I looked over my "pattern" of guys—the strong, handsome, silent type who turned out to be about as deep as a puddle and incapable of a deep, loving relationship. I was (and I hate this cliché, but clichés are clichés for a reason) judging a book by its cover, over and over again.

I finally broke up with Jim, who then began to stalk me. Funny, he hardly wanted anything to do with me when I was dating him, but as soon as I broke up with him, he couldn't stay away. Nice.

I hated going through all that pain and hell. I hated having to tell people, "I'm divorced." In fact, my mother was so embarrassed and disappointed in me that she didn't tell anyone in Chippewa, until finally the neighbors became suspicious as to why I kept visiting without my husband. I hated admitting to myself that my next major love interest was a sex-addict, and the one after that was a stalker. But—and I'm sure you're ready for it now—here's the miracle part.

I look at my divorce and my subsequent stupid relationships this way. Had I not gone through all the pain and hell, had I not learned the hard way, down to my very core, what I really needed and wanted from a love relationship, I never would have been ready for The One. I wouldn't have recognized him if he came up and hit me on the head with Cupid himself. I literally had to get all the "Bills" out of my system to make room for …

Dave. Yup. My Happy Meal. He'd been there all along as my coworker and eventually good friend—while I was dating the stalker. Now, Dave *is* tall and handsome (and has the best butt in a pair of Levis), but he's probably the whitest person I've ever seen. There's nothing dark and mysterious about him. But he makes me laugh. He skips without restraint. He respects me and listens to me, and I am myself with him 100 percent of the time. He loves me for me. He loves my friends and family. And I know he'd do anything in the world for me.

He made me a cover for my book and gave it to me for New Year's because he believes in miracles. He believes in me.

Now, I wouldn't wish divorce (or Pete or Jim) on anyone. But as I look back, I can honestly say I would not be as happy or fulfilled as I am today had I not gone through that. So, if you are divorced or have been in bad relationships (and who hasn't?), look at it this way. You can drag them around like an anchor and curse your bad luck or the significant others themselves—and then drag all that baggage into your next relationship. Or you can look at them for what they taught you, bless them for that, and move on, knowing that it's part of your unique journey to becoming who you really are: a self that you can authentically share with someone else—ultimately, the *right* someone else. That's the miracle of it all. If it took going through all that to get to where I am now, I'd do it all again. Sometimes miracles take a while, but they'll always take you to a better place.

"Getting Personal"

My best friend Sharon has also had her share of dates from hell. Two of her high school boyfriends turned out to be gay. Not that there's anything wrong with that. It just would have been nice to know, so she wouldn't spend years thinking there was something wrong with her because they wouldn't kiss her. Then there was her college boyfriend, Matt. Man, was *he* a hottie! Washboard abs, big muscular thighs, a butt you could bounce a quarter off of, and a face that shaving cream commercials would fight over. *Yummm.*

Unfortunately, he got "roid rage" when his dreams of becoming an NFL player were benched—not a pretty sight (or a safe one, either), no matter how hunky he was. So, after a couple of incredible-hulk tirades, Sharon decided looks weren't everything and got the hell outta there. Next up was the really nice, rich, but *waaay* unattractive guy whom Sharon thought she could fall in love with, even though he physically repulsed her and had just one testicle. And finally, there was the blind date with the Marine who said, "If you won't do it for me, do it for your country." Really. You can't make this shit up.

So when the local paper advertised a Pre-Valentine's Day Single's Party, Sharon wasn't exactly rushing to sign up. But her friend Deborah absolutely *begged* her to go. She was divorced and was more hopeful, i.e., inexperienced, about the dating world than Sharon. So Sharon, being the good friend she is, agreed to go, thinking at the very least she could protect Deborah from what she'd already been through.

It was February 12, 1998. As soon as they got to the party, a guy named David who had flipped up the collar of his suit jacket (remember, this was *not* the '80s) immediately homed in on them. "Hi, I'm David. I'm a thirty-four-year-old, single male ..." *Oh, God,* Sharon thought. A walking singles ad. It was that bad.

To bide her time and avoid eye contact with everyone, Sharon decided to try her hand at the free personal ad offered by the newspaper just for coming to the party. "Describe yourself," it said, "and what you're looking for."

Anyone who's not insane, came to mind, but in order to be interesting, even optimistic, she wrote, "I'm looking for a Renaissance Man." She described herself as a woman who was "just as comfortable watching a football game as I am wearing long skirts, capes, and corsets during the Renaissance Festival."

The next step, after she got home, was to create her voice-mail box so that "hot guys could call" her. Here's how she described *that* process:

"The system would ask a question, and I'd answer. I think the deal was that the voice-mail gods would put all my answers together in one big piece, making me sound either really interesting or horribly verbose. I had a horrible cold, so I think I had that Brenda Vaccaro voice thing going. I think only three people called me: a short, Asian, volleyball-playing atheist (huh?), a trader of some sort who worked at the Minneapolis Grain Exchange and said he wore a blazing-orange jacket so people would notice him (strike number two), and a guy named Todd. When I got Todd's message, I played it for Janelle and Deborah at work. I thought his voice was sexy."

Todd was the only guy she called back. Phone tag ensued.

"Once Todd and I finally spoke, I had to tell him I was leaving town for over a week for work with a group taking a cruise in the Caribbean." (Sharon works for a travel incentive company). "We got together probably three weeks later at a local Irish bar and sat and talked for about five hours. In spite of the fact that he was (and still is) a Deadhead, we hit it off quite well."

Their schedules kept them apart in the beginning. But Sharon says she knew he was The One the first night he kissed her—not just because of the kiss, which was great, but also because of the calm and collected way that he subsequently handled the drunk woman resembling Shelley Winters (at her Poseidon-Adventure weight) who backed into Sharon's car. Oh, and there was the fact that he laughed for half an hour straight when she bought a can of Spaghettios for dinner at Super America.

Not gay. No roid rage. And certainly not ugly (and with both testicles intact). He had no bad lines or flipped-up collars. He was normal, intelligent, good-looking, and he just loved Sharon for being Sharon.

Well, Todd did turn out to be The One. How he and Sharon even met is nothing short of a miracle. Todd *never* read, let alone answered, personal ads. And Sharon *never* wrote them, except for that one time. And Sharon *never* would have gone to that singles party where she wrote the ad if Deborah hadn't begged and pleaded and guilted her into going.

And what if Sharon had gone ahead and married that really, really nice but oh-so-not-attractive guy? What then? It boggles the mind.

Sharon and Todd were married exactly two years to the day after the Pre-Valentine's Day Singles Party that brought them together: February 12, 2000. And I'm happy to say that they are living happily ever after.

"The Buckeye"

This story is about a miracle in a nutshell. Literally.

I think I must have been about eighteen years old when Dad gave me his lucky buckeye. You know, one of those round, brown, chestnut-type things that have a light-tan circle at each end? It's about the size of a big marble.

Anyway, it was before I left for college when Dad held his hand over mine and said, "This is for good luck and protection." Apparently he'd carried it in his pocket for that very reason for years, and he wanted to pass its good karma on to me as I embarked on my adult life. I thought it was cool, and yes, I did carry it with me. After all, if a World War II and Korean War veteran thought this little nut had something to do with his survival, who was I to argue? But I didn't realize its significance until many years later.

As a journalist, I'd been in many dangerous places and situations: crossing the Hungarian-Czechoslovakian border when the Gulf War broke out in 1990 (let's just say the Eastern Bloc wasn't too friendly to Americans); Cali, Colombia, at a time when Americans were routinely abducted and held for ransom or sold into white slavery; even North Minneapolis after a white cop shot a black teenager and riots left news vehicles in flames. Yes, I'd carried my buckeye, out of habit more than fear. I suppose it could have had something to do with my staying safe. But as I said, that wasn't *the* significance of it, big-picture-wise. That came on Christmas nearly twenty years later.

I'd started working with Dave that year. He was a photojournalist at the station I worked for, and we were a good team. I knew enough about shooting to be of help to him in the field; he knew enough about writing to help me craft some attention-grabbing lines. But I also felt a "connection" with him, something deeper and more meaningful than the rush of a good news story. It could have been a crush, I thought. But I was in a relationship (not a great one, by any means), and he was in the midst of a terrible divorce. So we limited ourselves to lamenting our respective love lives during long rides in the news car, turning out great reports in the process.

Well, my then-boyfriend turned out to be a heartless jerk, and Dave's divorce finally became final. So, we gradually started hanging out together after work, then seeing each other on weekends and going out on dates. Never before had I had such a deep connection with and feelings for anyone. Still, we were both gun-shy from our previous relationship debacles. So we moved very slowly. Hopefully, but slowly.

Christmas was fast approaching. We'd each made plans to visit family and then celebrate Christmas together when we returned. We agreed that big presents weren't appropriate; and we weren't to spend a lot of money.

So, when our "Christmas" came, he came over to my house and held out his hand. In it lay a tiny silver-wrapped box no bigger than your thumb. I knew it wasn't a ring. First, we weren't "there" yet in our relationship; second, no ring (at least not one with a stone of any size) would even fit in that box. So I was especially intrigued as to what was in there—not to mention how the heck he'd wrapped the wee thing!

Gently, gingerly, I untied the tiny bow and unfolded the tiny corners that formed the box. It lay open to reveal ...

A buckeye.

A buckeye! Now, I remember showing Dave my buckeye while we were out on shoots; telling him the story of how Dad gave it to me and how it was supposed to bring me good luck. I had even lent it to him as he was going through his messy divorce. But this wasn't that buckeye.

It turned out that when Dave went home for Christmas, he happened to go into his sister's basement—which he'd done a gazillion times over the years—and there in the middle of the floor lay one buckeye. No one knew how it had gotten there. There were no other buckeyes to be found anywhere. But there it was. He decided then and there that it was meant for him to give to me.

And when I saw that buckeye, I knew. I knew it was a sign from my Dad that this guy, this wonderful man, was The One. Dad was giving me that buckeye for "luck and protection," and it was his way, in death, of communicating to me that this was the soul meant for me, the soul that would bring me the luck and protection and happiness my father wanted for his daughter. And from his side of heaven, this was his way of letting me know.

I choose to think of it that way, anyway. Dave and I have been married for ten years now. We have two beautiful daughters, in addition to his great son Ryan. Every year on our anniversary we thank my Dad for helping bring us together.

And I still carry the buckeye.

"The Dance"

It was 1990. I was driving down the Kennedy Expressway in Chicago in my fire-engine-red Toyota Celica on my way to a client meeting, listening to country music. I was about to hear the song that would, in many ways, define my life from then on.

The song was "The Dance" written by Tony Arata and performed by Garth Brooks. If you've never heard it, find it. It's not only got the most beautiful, simply haunting melody but also the kind of message we all could use now and then: the importance of appreciating what *is* right now and blessing what *was*—even if it ended before you wanted it to.

"The Dance" brought me one of my first relationship miracles, although I was hard-pressed to call it that at the time . Tickets for Garth Brooks' upcoming concert in Chicago were about to go on sale. My then-husband Bill wasn't a Garth fan, but my girlfriend Jill was, so she offered to go stand in line way early in the morning to get us some tickets. For some reason, Bill drove me there later—just in time for her to race away from the ticket window screaming, "We got seventh row center!" I ran to her and nearly knocked her down with a hug; then we locked elbows and began to do our best "Wizard of Oz" skip back to the car, singing, "We got seventh row *cen*-ter; we got seventh row *cen*-ter!"

I was so happy—until Bill grabbed me by the elbow and shushed me, saying, "Stop it! People will *see* you!" What? Yes, it might be a little extreme for a couple of twenty-eight-year-olds to be skipping over tickets to a Garth Brooks concert, but it wasn't like we were holding up traffic or drawing a crowd or anything. But Bill would have none of it. We were *embarrassing* him.

To quote comedian Bill Engvall, "There's your sign."

It was during my divorce (no, it wasn't just because of the skipping incident, but that certainly was a sign) that "The Dance" came to mind again—this time when my dad died.

Dad had been diagnosed with lung cancer after forty-some years of smoking. I remember my phone ringing at 7:30 a.m. on June 13th. It was my brother calling to tell me that Dad had died at home sometime during the night.

For as close as Dad and I were, you'd think I'd have dissolved into tears. But I got up, almost robotically, and put Garth's CD into my boom box. I skipped ahead to "The Dance" and put it on repeat, and then took out several pictures of my Dad.

Over and over again, as I sat cross-legged on the floor with pictures scattered all around me, the words of "The Dance" meant more to me than ever. Had I known, and had Dad known, how his life would end and how soon, we would have missed all of the precious times we'd had together, worrying about the future. As it was, we enjoyed the special father-daughter connection we had right up until the end. We didn't have any unfinished business. Our time wasn't tarnished by obsessing over the future. It was, authentically, our "dance." And though I never wanted Dad to die, I wouldn't have missed our dance—just the way it was—for anything.

Fast-forward to one of my subsequent attempts at having a successful relationship with Bill—only this time his name was Jim. Give me an "A" for effort, because I really tried to reform this Bill-clone into relationship material. I took up golf. I hate golf. And skiing. I'm terrified of skiing. All in an attempt to appreciate *his* world so he would repay in kind. Here's where "The Dance" came in again (thank God that He's patient).

Once again, Garth Brooks was coming to town. This time it was in Minneapolis. And again, I could not get to the ticket place first thing in the morning because I had to work. So I asked Jim if he would go get us tickets. His response? "I'm not getting up early on a Saturday morning to go stand in line for some dumb country music concert."

There's your sign.

I was heartbroken. Through all my years of hardship, divorce, Dad dying, changing jobs, and moving several times, Garth's music, specifically "The Dance," had been my constant. It kept me appreciating what I had and blessing my learning experiences, even when they caused me pain. I felt a need to go to the concert. But as I sat looking at videotape at the TV station that morning, I resigned myself to the realization that I probably wouldn't be able to go.

Enter Dave. Dave and I worked together on Saturdays a lot of the time. He was one of my favorite news photographers to work with. We really clicked. That morning, he had been sent down to the Target Center to shoot the long line for the Garth Brooks concert tickets. Unfortunately, I hadn't been sent with him.

I was sitting at the editing deck, looking at tape, when Dave walked in the back door of the station. He always had a great smile and twinkly eyes when he saw me, but this time he was extra bubbly. He said, "Hey, I got something for you." He reached in his pocket and pulled out two tickets to the Garth Brooks concert. "Here," he said, "I got these for you and Jim."

I couldn't believe it. I had mentioned to Dave how much I loved Garth and how I'd wanted to go to the concert. He said he'd shot the long lines getting tickets, and when he was done, he simply went up to the ticket window to see whether any tickets were left. There were, so he bought them. For me and Jim.

There's your sign.

I dumped Jim and took Dave.

Then, the first time Dave came to my townhouse, we decided to listen to music in my living room. I turned on the radio, and what was the first song to play, right as I turned it on?

"The Dance."

Just in case I hadn't gotten it the first three times, there was my sign. We danced to it in the middle of my living room floor. I could feel my Dad smiling. I felt that same peace that I'd felt when looking at his photographs in my apartment in Chicago. I knew, at that moment, that Dave was sent to continue The Dance with me for the rest of my life.

So, yes, I could have missed the pain (of Bill, Jim, etc., etc.) but I'd have had to miss the ultimate dance … with Dave.

"Wedding Miracles"

Getting married at age thirty-seven (and for the second time) is much different from getting married in your twenties. In many ways, I found it less angst-ridden. I knew myself better; I knew my husband-to-be better; I was established in my career and had friends who had proven themselves to be in it for the long haul. I could show up in jeans and a T-shirt and serve cheeseburgers at my wedding, and they'd still all come and be fine with that. So that kind of pressure was off.

The harder part was that, at age thirty-seven, I had more responsibilities and less flexibility (and less money) for the whole wedding-planning frenzy. I didn't have time to research dates and locations, to compare florists' prices or sample wedding cake. Dave had his baggage too. Because he was Catholic—but had gotten a divorce and was about to marry a Lutheran—well, he wasn't allowed anywhere near a Catholic church ceremony. I wasn't attached to any church (by choice) and quickly found that, in order to get married in any of the ones I called, we'd have to become members beforehand. Since we're really not church-goers, that seemed kind of hypocritical. So we decided to have a judge marry us in a nonreligious location. Easy, right?

The Judge: Dave and I knew of one judge who had married some acquaintances of ours. He was an old Wilford Brimley-type with a storyteller's voice who now, in his older years, wore flannel shirts and fished a lot. Dave and I made an appointment to meet him at a nearby Perkins restaurant after work one night. That's when the "judge saga" began.

When we walked into Perkins in our Channel 5 winter jackets (it was January, so we all had to be branded in Channel 5 winter gear), the old judge immediately fell pale. He was polite and listened to our plans, but he made an excuse to leave a little too soon and then called and said he wouldn't be available to do our wedding. Ever. Little did we know that several years back the old judge had been exposed by Channel 5 for allegedly trolling for prostitutes along Lake Street in Minneapolis. There had been a big scandal; he was never formally charged, but he had "retired" from the bench shortly thereafter. So when Dave and I walked into Perkins in our Channel 5 jackets, the judge thought we were an undercover news crew coming after him again. Poor old guy. We really did just want to get married. But we couldn't convince him, and we wound up having to launch another search for a judge without any skeletons (or prostitutes) in the closet.

The Location and Date: Where does an "older" couple hold their second wedding if not in a church? There we sat in January, pondering popular landmarks, hotels, friends' houses, and courthouses. And then there was the problem of *when*. Because we were in news, we couldn't take off during ratings months. So that took February, May, September, and November out of the running. And also because we were in news, money was definitely a limitation. We'd pick a date, and the places we liked would be booked. If we looked for new locations that were available on our chosen dates, they'd be too expensive. Living in sin would have been an option, save for the fact that Dave had a six-year-old son whose father preferred to be a role model. So that was out.

All we needed was a miracle. Now, I admit, none of these roadblocks were dire. I can't remember turning all bridezilla and stressing about "my day" never happening. But I did realize that everything we were trying wasn't working—like when you have to work too hard to make a relationship work, and it never does. So we decided to let go and let the answers come to us. And suddenly ...

Why not Sunday? Dave and I had exhausted every possible Saturday in 2001. I remember sitting on the floor of my townhouse, not worrying about it, when all of a sudden I thought, *What about Sunday?* Were there any Sundays that stood out? I looked at the calendar. August 26th was the day that Dave and I had first seen the Northern Lights together while we were on that inspiring story in Rochester. *Sunday, August 26th.* Of course! We started to look at our options on *that* day.

We loved the outdoors and had even considered having our wedding on a boat. But the boat we wanted to rent—one that could accommodate about a hundred guests—was too expensive on a Saturday. But on Sunday, August 26th, not only was it available; it was less expensive. *Booked!*

The Judge, again: The second judge referred to us by some friends had not been available on the Saturdays we wanted; but she was available on Sunday, the 26th. *Booked!*

The Music: We were on a roll. So we decided to continue on and just tap the resources we were familiar with from our past as a couple. Music? We couldn't afford a band, and somehow a DJ seemed a little cheesy for two people nearing forty. But when Dave, Ryan, and I went to our one-and-only wedding fair, we heard an announcement over the loudspeaker that caught our attention. The local musician/composer we had done a story with ("Warm Hands, Cold Heart"), Steven C. Anderson, was performing over in "aisle such-and-such." Steven had been amazing, and the story we'd done with him about how he composed a song for a little boy who had died had left an impression in our hearts. Immediately Dave and I walked over to him and reintroduced ourselves. He remembered us and called Ryan over to let him play his piano. "Do you do weddings?" we asked. "I do weddings," he answered. His rate was affordable compared to a band, and—as luck (or miracles) would have it—he was available on Sunday, August 26th. *Booked!*

And so it went. I could go on about the series of miracles that fell into place: the one-stop shopping for a dress, the news photographers who volunteered to shoot our wedding, and the bakery that agreed to do a simple, affordable cake in the shape of an angel without making me feel like an idiot. But it was the lesson of letting go that set the miracles in motion.

For years, I had forced relationships into working. But as it turned out, the only relationships that really *did* work were the ones I didn't force: Dave, Sharon, etc. Once I realized that, "let go," and stopped forcing my wedding as well, everything that was meant-to-be fell into place. Okay, so it took me thirty-seven years, one failed marriage, and countless other dead-end relationships to figure that out, but I got it. And it resulted in a miraculous, unforgettable wedding that was uniquely ours—and effortless—because of the miracle of *not* working at it.

We made it!
Dave and me on our honeymoon in British Columbia.

How to See Miracles in Your Own Relationships

Whether they're in your past, present, or future, relationships always have been and will continue to be messy. Friends will piss you off. Boyfriends and girlfriends will hurt you. Parents will screw up. Kids will alternately thrill and disappoint you. But the miracles show up when you look at relationships this way: with compassion. Most of the time, people are doing the best they can with what they have (and know) at the time, yourself included. Recognizing this leads to forgiveness and—another way to look at them—appreciation. Even the relationships that hurt or fail can contribute to your being a better, more knowledgeable person today. Think about it. Are you proud of the person you are today? Do you have better relationships now because of what you went through in the past? If you and your mom didn't get along, think of how that can impact how you parent your own children. You'll try to do better. If you've gone through a divorce, think of what you've learned that you'll do differently next time. Every relationship is an opportunity for growth, and without each one, you would not be the person you are today.

Chapter Six: Pet Miracles

I Like to Think of Pets as Four-Legged Angels …

… who are here to remind us how to see miracles in what we would consider the mundane.

About my dog Max: it didn't matter whether I was away from him for eight hours or eight minutes; every time I came home, he about turned himself inside out with waggles and woofs in unbridled—or rather, unmuzzled—joy.

And every time I said, "Wanna go for a walk?" from the time he was a pup until he died at age thirteen, you'd have thought he'd won the Super Lotto. "*Oh-my-God. A walk!* Oh boy, oh boy, oh boy!"

I don't have as much experience with cats, but I remember my grandma's cat Dusty sitting mesmerized for hours, watching the birds outside the window—same window, same bird action, day in and day out. But it never got old to her. Occasionally, she'd swat at the window and meow, like she was some badass protecting my grandma's house from evil sparrows. But mostly, she just hung out there, happy for the occasional scratch and to curl up at my grandma's fee at the end of every day. To me, she represented living, breathing contentment.

Joy, love, and appreciation for what you have. Pets live it in our presence every day. I think they see the world the way God sees it and would like us to see it: new and full of possibilities every day.

My miracles "tour guide," Max, on during one of our many
hikes by Split Rock Lighthouse near Duluth.

"The Walk"

Oprah would call this an "Aha!" moment.

Thank God, or else it would have just been a freeze-my-ass-off-for-no-good-reason moment.

I was walking my Airedale terrier Max. Actually, it was so cold that I *drove* Max the four measly blocks or so to the trail he liked, and *then* got out for a walk. I remember opening my car door and stepping out into blinding white light, the kind where the sun and the snow are the same color and just bounce the freezing wind back and forth like a tennis ball. It was so bright-white for a moment that I thought I was having a near-death experience. The next moment I thought, *I'm so cold that that dying wouldn't be half bad.* But then my irises had squeezed to the size of pinholes and I could see again, there was the same old long (longer when it's cold) trail that Max adored, the one I picked because it allowed for "scoopless pooping," where I didn't have to pick up after him and then carry a bag of poop around for the entire walk (although frozen poop doesn't smell as bad).

Max bounded out of the car like it was the best day of his life. When his paws hit the snow, he hunkered down and spun round and round, nose to tail, snow clumps shooting in all directions and all over me, in his happy doggy dance. I remember shaking my head at him, all crabby and cold with icicles forming on my eyelashes. "Max, we've been on this trail four zillion times. Just hurry up and go to the bathroom." (I always talked to Max, even though I firmly believe that what he heard was more like that *Far Side* cartoon where the dog's owner is going on and on, and all that the dog hears is "Blah blah blah, Max, blah blah, Max …") Anyway, I grumbled, why all the excitement over the *same* trees, *same* lake, *same* inhumane Minnesota cold, *same* everything every day?

Then, Aha!

I realized for the first time that Max didn't see it that way. Although he knew the trail by heart, he always expected—and seemed to find—something new to appreciate about it. Maybe a new smell, a new drift of snow to plow through, another tree in which the birds would hide until Max could flush them out. He approached the trail—and really, every day—with fresh eyes (and fresh snout). Where I saw only routine and monotony, he saw opportunity. And walk after walk after walk, he always came back happily satisfied with what he'd discovered that day.

It occurred to me that maybe that's how God would like us to see the world, with every day a fresh start, a fresh opportunity to find—and do—something good in it. He did say something about how we should receive the kingdom of God like little children, full of wonder and excitement and appreciation. That morning I decided that He probably was referring to how pets receive the kingdom too.

Suddenly the trail and the day looked new and exciting to me too. I just had to see it through Max's eyes. Maybe that's why God sends us dogs: to help us calm our busy minds and really see the miracles all around us.

"The Max-Tree"

I never wanted to believe that Max would die. He had been with me for nearly fourteen years. Through four jobs, six moves, and two husbands, he was my rock. I can still see his inky-black eyes loving me, adoring me at times when no one else seemed to. Not even me. But there he was, all fur and four legs and love, always.

My first husband and I got Max about a year after we got married. Bill had always wanted an Airedale; he had fond memories of playing with his family Airedale, Annie, when he was a boy. I just loved dogs, period, so I was okay with any breed we got.

We met Max's brother first. "Sam" was at a party one of our friends was having. He was an adorable fuzz of a puppy. Airedales are nearly all black when they're born, save for a little tan mask around their tiny black eyes; and their fur sprays out from around their noses and eyes like a fireworks surprise. With their round little bellies and awkward paws, they just couldn't be any cuter. So when our friend told us that "Sam" had a brother and sister left in the litter, Bill and I couldn't resist.

The next day we drove out to the farm to meet Sam's siblings. As we got out of the car, two little balls of fuzz scampered around the corner of the farmhouse and skidded to a stop at our feet. There they were, Max and his sister, all tongues and happy yips. I knelt down to play with them, upon which they belly-flopped over and offered me squirmy tummies to scratch. I could smell that sweet puppy smell as their needle-teeth nipped at my fingertips. I was immediately knee-deep in puppy love.

Bill seemed equally enamored with both of them. As he got on with the business of talking dollars with the breeder, I looked at the pups more closely. They were both adorable, both well-behaved and healthy. But the little boy pup—I don't know. It felt like I knew him, somehow, somewhere. When he looked at me, I just felt that unmistakable "it" that says, in rare situations, "This is the one." (It's the same voice I *hadn't* listened to when I got married, the one that said, "This isn't the one." But that's another story.)

So when Bill asked me which one I thought we should take, I picked the pup that we would eventually name Max—short for his full, registered name: "Maxwell, Duke of Rochester." The name was very regal, very "un-Max-like," since he was all snuggles and friendliness and never did walk well on a leash.

What Max *did* do well was to model a kind of unconditional love, patience, and appreciation of life that guided me through the best and hardest times. We took a million long walks together, during which he helped me see the many miracles of nature: the glee of bounding through tall grasses, the excitement of snuffling the scents of the latest critter passerby, the sleepy comfort of spring sunshine on your skin (or fur), the endless adventure in what might be buried under the latest snowfall. He got me "out" on the days when all I wanted to do was burrow under my covers and feel sorry for myself, like during my divorce. He was such a source of strength for me that of all the "assets" Bill and I shared, it was Max that I fought for. I couldn't bear the thought of another woman having a relationship with my dog.

Max never complained, acted out, or judged me (or any of the lackluster guys I introduced him to). He simply stayed by my side, offering up his thick, curly fur for me to hold on to and, many times, to cry into. If I had paid better attention, I would have noticed how he never really took to any of the guys I dated (there's your sign) until I found Dave. From the moment Dave walked through my door, Max greeted him with waggles and licks and love, as if to say "*There* you are! We've been waiting for you!"

Max lived long enough to get me married to Dave and help us move into the house we would call home, the one in which we would raise our children. By then he was thirteen, and while I knew he was well past the age most Airedales live, I couldn't even fathom his not being with me. When I became pregnant with my first child, Samantha, I looked forward to his being by my side for yet another milestone in my life, just as he had been for the past thirteen years.

Seven months into my pregnancy, Max's old, furry body began to shut down. Our walks got much slower and shorter. He slept more and ate less. He began to pant, as though it was hard for him to breathe. Then on one night in April, he padded into our bedroom, panting loudly enough that it woke us up. When I turned on the light, I could see that he was bleeding slightly from his nose and mouth. He seemed apologetic as I hoisted him into the car and on to the emergency room. Quietly, strongly, I sat by his side as the veterinarian tried to figure out what was wrong.

The next couple of days are a blur. I think I've kept them that way because the experience of Max dying is still too painful to relive on any level. I'll do my best here to describe his final days … but forgive me if I can't linger on the details. The simple fact was that his blood wasn't clotting anymore. We took him to the University of Minnesota veterinary hospital, where they detected a large mass in his belly and other organs. With fluids and oxygen, he seemed to rally for a short time, but while I was on my way to visit him, he suffered a stroke.

When I got there, he was on his side, eyes barely open and barely alive. The veterinarian said they could open him up to see what was wrong, but that the surgery likely would kill him. Either way, his quality of life would not return to any real level of quality. Trying to be the source of strength that he had been for me for so many years, I had them wrap him up in a blanket and bring him outside to the garden so I could just sit with him in the sunlight under the trees, talk to him, and say good-bye.

Dave came from work, and together we held and petted him, went through our many memories together, thanked him, and comforted him. At some point, Max seemed to completely relax, as though he was telling me it was all right, that he was ready. Still trying to be strong, I had everyone put him in my arms so I could be with him when he died. The vet caringly administered the medicine that "put him to sleep." I told him I loved him as he died peacefully in my arms.

A couple of weeks after Max died, we decided to hold a ceremony to remember him. I went to the nursery and wandered around until I found a dogwood tree whose scraggly this-way-and-that branches reminded me of Max's fur and spontaneous fun demeanor, and I brought it home. Our closest friends came and stood around in a circle with me, while Dave dug a hole in our backyard, a spot with a good view of the pond, to plant the Max-tree in. In the bottom of the hole, we placed some of Max's ashes, a rawhide bone, and some cheese (Max's favorite); and as we took turns throwing soil back around the tree's roots, we each said a few words about what this wonderful being had meant to us. Max had touched so many lives with love and laughter. I still couldn't believe that he was gone.

I visited the Max-tree several times before our first baby was born. I would hold the tips of its wee branches between my fingers and stroke them like I used to stroke that special spot behind his right ear. I'd talk to him, tell him how much I missed him and how I wished he were there to welcome our baby home. I asked that he watch over her as she came into this world and be her "angel dog." Maybe he already knew her, I fancied. Maybe he'd be the one making sure she got here all right.

And she did. All seven pounds and one ounce of her. Baby Samantha was born on May 30th, scrappy and happy. My labor was blessedly easy. But as we neared the discharge from the hospital, I worried about being home. Yes, I had all the standard worries of a new parent. (*Now* what do I do? Where is the instruction manual?) But I also had the fear of returning to a house without Max. Somehow, he made every place "home" for me. And my grief over losing him was still fresh. How was I supposed to raise a baby without his trusting eyes willing me onward?

Dave and I drove about three miles per hour all the way home from the hospital. It was a warm, breezy day with the sun gently stroking our skin the way it does when summer is new. Of course, it didn't keep us from bundling Sam up like an Eskimo for the excursion, but it was a great day to welcome our new baby home.

After we stumbled into the house amidst picture-taking and diaper bags, Dave went out to cut some fresh lilacs from the yard to have at my side while I breastfed Sam. He came back all excited, saying, "You've got to come see!"

He took me out the sliding glass door into our backyard and pointed. I squinted as I nestled Sam under one arm and held the other up to shield my eyes from the sun. And there, in its tiny corner of our yard, stood the Max tree, full of blossoms! Blossoms that hadn't been there when we'd left for the hospital two days earlier. Blossoms that I knew were there to welcome our little girl home.

That's when I knew that Max really hadn't left me at all. In the same way that I "knew" he was the puppy to take home that day thirteen years before. I "knew" he had become an angel—probably timed just right to meet Sam, teach her a few things, then guide her on down safely to me in this world. As always, Max was taking care of me. My four-legged guardian angel was now my daughter's.

"The Head Hug"

Our daughter, Alex, at her pre-Kindergarten "graduation:"
one of many times I got Alex's loving "head hug."

If you've ever had an Airedale, one thing you learn early on is that they have a really heavy, hard head. You learn that by getting whacked on your own head as you lovingly bend down to scratch their ears. Then, *thunk!* You're seeing those little birdies fly around your head as you try and regain consciousness.

Max was no different. "Ooooohhhh, good puppy … *Thwack!*" "Such a good boy … *Thud.*" It took nearly getting several black eyes and biting my tongue off before I learned the bob-and-weave technique necessary to effectively pet and scratch my dog.

One other thing that Max did with his "anvil head," besides beat me with it, was hug—me, my friend, my husband, anyone he loved (which was just about everyone). If you were standing, he'd plow his head between your knees and just stand there. If you were sitting, he'd sit down next to you and lean his head back on your thigh with rapture. Crouch down, and he'd lean into you with his head. Unlike his well-intentioned head butts, these head-hugs were not dangerous and remain one of the many things I miss about Max.

Fast-forward to nearly three years after Max died. Our first daughter Sam had always seemed to have an awareness of Max, even though he died nearly two months before she was born. She always talked to him and told the "Max-tree" she missed him. Now there was little Alex too, who was almost a year old. I always thought that she was probably born too long after Max's death to have that same awareness or "feel" him in any way. Then came … the head hug.

The first time it happened, I think it was when Dave was carrying Alex downstairs. She had just gotten up from a nap and didn't know I was down in the kitchen. As I came around the corner and smiled at her, she dove—literally *dove*—headfirst at me. It wasn't the reaching kind of dive that babies do for their mommies; it only involved her head. That time I wrote it off simply as one of those things babies do to give you nightmares of them tumbling down a flight of stairs or out of their high chairs, head first into oblivion. But then it happened again the next day at Debbie's when we picked her up at daycare. Again, no arms, just the head hug as Debbie handed her to me. She did the same thing with Dave. And as soon as she started walking, she began planting her head in between my legs to "hug" me, just like Max used to do. Call me crazy (and I'm sure you have, by now), but I like to think it's Max's way of saying "hello" and that he's taking care of Baby Alex too, channeling head hugs through her. Sometimes I'll scratch Alex behind her ear—my way of saying "hi" and "thank you, Max" right back. I love you, Max.

"Rudy"

I've wanted to get another Airedale ever since Max died. When the girls were three and four and an opportunity to get a puppy came our way, I thought it must be time. But we were just one stop on Rudy's miracle journey.

When I was a reporter, I interviewed a government official who turned out to be an Airedale-lover like I was. Max was still alive at the time, and he was a breeder; so whenever I saw him, we shared stories about our Airedales and what a cool breed they were.

One day, about a year after I left channel 5, "Tom" got in touch with me and said they had a new litter of pups and would we be interested in having one. Dave and I were working out of our home at the time, and the girls were up and walking, so I thought, why not? We drove up to his farm in Brainerd, Minnesota, to meet the mom and her litter.

And of course, if you've ever seen Airedale puppies, you know you're pretty much toast from the minute they scamper out from wherever they are to wiggle and waggle at your feet. With their fuzzy coats and ink-black eyes and noses, they look like stuffed animals filled with nothing but cuteness and love. Their mom was beautiful, a big girl with a beautiful coat and sweet disposition. Their dad was some god-like champion in the Airedale world. How could we go wrong? I scooped up the little male puppy who was worming his way in and out of my legs and into my heart and took out our checkbook.

We named him Rudy after the soundtrack that was playing in our car on the two-hour car ride home. "Rudy" was the name of a Notre Dame legend whose life's dream was to play for the Fighting Irish, but he didn't have the size or the grades to ever really have a chance. Until he did. Through perseverance, faith, and failure (and quite a bit of scrappiness), he got into Notre Dame and onto the football field for the last series of the last game—in which he made a winning tackle. Not a bad namesake for a puppy, we thought. So Rudy it was.

Well, Rudy embodied only a couple of his namesake's traits, and even those presented themselves in an unexpected way. He was scrappy to the core—into everything to the point of destruction—and he persevered, despite every ounce of obedience training, treats, and scolding we could muster. And in terms of size, he definitely was no Rudy. By eight months he weighed in at nearly eighty pounds and was taller than both of our girls. I felt like we were living our own version of Alice in Wonderland where she outgrew her own house. Neither Dave nor I could handle him inside or outside the house. Don't get me wrong. He wasn't mean. He was just an enormous, curious, energetic puppy. We actually took him to a dog boarding kennel one weekend because we needed to repair our home and figure out what the hell we were going to do with him.

He made our decision for us that spring when we were outside in the yard, playing with the girls. Rudy had taken to running in circles around the house, which we were glad about because he might burn off some energy and be somewhat manageable when we went back inside. But on his last pass, Rudy jumped up playfully on our daughter Sam from behind, sending her flying face-first onto our cement driveway. One bloody nose and cut lip later, we decided to find Rudy another home.

I called the breeder, Tom, to see whether he could take Rudy back. They had another litter on the way, he said, but let him see what he could do. That's when our place in Rudy's journey became clear.

Less than one day later, Tom called back and said that right after we had called he'd received a call from another Airedale owner, Wendy, who had raised two of his puppies—siblings—for nearly ten years. She was devastated because one of the two had just died, and her remaining Airedale, Chelsea, was beside herself with loneliness. Did he have any Airedales that she could adopt to be Chelsea's companion?

Tom's puppies wouldn't be born for a few more weeks, and Chelsea needed something older than a new puppy anyway. Wendy lived up in Brainerd, alone save for her dogs, on a large piece of land near a lake where the dogs could have the run of the place. She *loved* and pampered her dogs. Tom thought Rudy might be exactly what she needed.

When we called Wendy, she about jumped through the phone. It was a miracle, she said, that we had called Tom right when she needed another dog. We arranged to drive Rudy up to meet her and see whether she wanted him. I felt bad; I'd never given up a dog before, and I so loved having a dog in my home. But we went for Rudy's sake and for our children's. Two hours later, we pulled into Wendy's long drive and saw a beautiful, wooded lot with a friendly (although overweight) old Airedale girl trotting down the lane to greet us. Carefully, we got out and unloaded our elephant-dog Rudy, whom she regarded with maternal curiosity.

When Wendy saw Rudy, she gasped at how beautiful he was. She was not deterred by his size or energy. In fact, she remarked how he'd bring new life into the place and might even help old Chelsea lose some weight. As we walked Rudy around her property and then her house, we saw that he would encounter love and room to grow. Rudy's excited snuffling at all the smells inside and out confirmed that he thought the place was great too. And although he perked his ears and tilted his head at us as we left him there, I knew he finally was where he was supposed to be.

That Christmas we got a card from Rudy (with the help of Wendy) who said that he loved his new home, that he went everywhere with Wendy and spent lots of time exploring the woods, swimming in the lake, and eating from the perpetually open bag of biscuits in Wendy's entryway. He said that Chelsea sometimes growled at him, but only when he wouldn't leave her alone for her daily nap. He included a picture; he must have gained another ten pounds or more since we'd last seen him, but he had that unmistakably happy Airedale face that I'd come to know and love with my own Airedale, Max.

So yes, we were supposed to have Rudy, but only temporarily until he got to his forever home with Wendy. I'm glad we were part of his miracle journey. Hopefully, someday, we'll be on the receiving end of another Airedale miracle of our own.

"Max, the Cat"

I've never been a cat person. I couldn't see the point. I mean, you give them a home, you feed them, you talk baby talk to them, and buy them silly toys; and then when you want to pet them and give them a little love, they just can't seem to be bothered. "Oh, *you* again? (sigh) Well, if you must. But I've got a sofa arm I have to scratch to hell in a minute, so get on with it." Whereas with dogs, you *know* they love you. My dog Max went berserk *every* time I'd walk in the door. I was the best thing since sliced bacon. The love just waggled out of him. Ever seen a cat do that? Me neither.

But my girls wanted a pet. It didn't help that I'd regularly take them to the Humane Society instead of the zoo because I was too lazy to drive the extra ten miles on a Saturday morning. We'd visit the kitties and the bunnies and the dogs. In and out in thirty minutes, tops, without spending a dime. Except that in about a week, they'd start talking about getting a pet again.

I knew that we couldn't handle a dog right then. With two working parents and three kids—ages sixteen, seven, and five—our schedules were too nuts. I had had my dog Max for nearly fourteen wonderful years, and I knew that a dog needed—and deserved—the kind of time, attention, exercise, and play that we didn't have time for. My husband, a cat owner in his previous marriage, said that cats were much less needy, and he would be fine with getting one if I thought the girls should have one. Still …

So, last Christmas I bought each of the girls one of those motion-activated cats that meows, washes itself, and turns its head to watch you as you go by. It'll even roll on its back and purr if you touched it a certain way. Kind of creepy, but I thought it was worth a shot. They were delighted—until the batteries wore out and the mechanical kitties took up residence in the crawl space under the house.

Fast-forward to the end of August. My older daughter Sam was invited to a Saturday morning birthday party. Alex, the younger one, was feeling sad because she wasn't invited, so I suggested we go see the pets at the Humane Society. We got there right when the doors opened. Alex, as usual, ran right into the cat room to play with the kittens. And as soon as she walked into the room, two little gray paws shot out of one of the bottom cages, followed by intense meowing from the owner of those paws. Alex knelt down and touched the kitten, a little gray number who had no outstanding characteristics except for his intense attraction to Alex. Every time she walked away, he'd begin the reaching and the meowing. She'd go back, and he'd settle down. It went on the entire time we were there. Finally, I decided to check him out myself: male, four months old, part of an unwanted litter, neutered, etc., all unremarkable … until I saw his name. *Max.*

After about a half hour, we left, just as we usually did. But I couldn't get that cat out of my head. At first I brushed it off to sentimentality, because I've never stopped missing my dog Max. But over the course of the next three weeks, I found myself regularly checking the Humane Society website to see if "Max" was still there. He was. Finally one night I said to Dave, "You know, I can't get that cat out of my head. Isn't that weird? I don't even *like* cats."

"Why don't you go get him?" Dave said.

"Really?"

So the next morning the girls and I went over to the Humane Society the minute it opened and went to see Max. Same reaction. Max reached out of the cage and arched up his back to be petted as soon as the girls came over. I asked one of the workers if we could get him out and take him into the visitation room. Once out and about, Max was playful and not too skittish. The girls were ecstatic. "Let's get him! Let's get him!"

So we did. After filling out enough paperwork for security clearance by the Secret Service, they put Max the Cat in a carrier box, and we brought him home. Once out of the box, I fully expected him to scoot under the sofa and not come out for days. But, no. After sniffing around—first the kitchen and then the rest of the house, room by room—Max contentedly adopted us, as though he belonged there and had simply been lending us the house until he arrived. Unlike other cats I've known, he's been playful, cuddly, talkative, and patient with the kids. He loves us and comes running when we get home. He sleeps with the girls every night. It's like he's always been here. Maybe he has.

The girls have since renamed the cat. First, they wanted to call him *Sarah*, which I promptly declined on the grounds that any male cat would find it insulting. Then they decided on *Cookie*, which I still think is a bit undignified, but he wears it well. But the fact that the cat's original name was Max is not lost on me. I believe it's Max's way of being with us—or taking care of us—in a way that we need right now.

"Poke-Along Contentedly"

When my brother Steve was in the Marine Corps, he and his wife got a basset hound puppy named Pokey, which was short for his AKC name: "Poke-Along Contentedly." Pokey was the embodiment of his name, all ears and paws and one pace: slow. I remember playing with him when Steve and his wife moved back to Chippewa into our grandma's old house. At some point during a subsequent move, Pokey came to live with my mom, dad, and me.

Now, Mom and Dad made no secret of the fact that they were long past having dogs in the house. They'd had them ever since we kids were little, to varying degrees of hassle and destruction in whatever home we were inhabiting at the time. There was a crazy boxer named

Rocket, who was a gem until the moment you left the house, at which time he would jump up on every bed in the house and pee on the pillows. There was Skoshi, who, in his sixteen or seventeen years on Earth, impregnated nearly every female dog in Chippewa at least once. This was no small feat, considering he was so short he'd get lost in the snowdrifts every winter. And then there was Boots, my dog, who had the embarrassing habit of rolling over and lying on his back in front of company with all of his junk hanging out.

No, Mom and Dad didn't miss having a dog. So when Pokey came, Dad wouldn't have a thing to do with him. He had his retired life just the way he wanted it: sedentary, quiet, and the same, day in and day out. Not the best for one's health, but neither Mom nor our family doctor nor anyone else was going to convince the old Marine otherwise.

Funny thing was, the more Dad ignored Pokey and went about his (lack of) business, the more Pokey took to him, following him around the house and "talking" at him with his "Yow-yow-yow-rrrr-rrr-rrr" signature growl. Reluctantly, Dad would pat him on the head or get him food or tell Mom or me to do it. But Pokey remained at Dad's heels, like he knew Dad needed to be bothered somehow, that his self-imposed retirement could use some tweaking.

And that's how—slowly (because that was Pokey's pace) and deliberately—Pokey's miracle unfolded. Pokey became the drill sergeant to Dad's nonmilitary retirement. Early every morning, Pokey padded upstairs to the foot of Dad's bed with his Yow-yow-yow-rrr-rrr-rrr version of reveille. That would get Dad up, dressed, and out the door for a morning stroll, which Dad never would have done on his own. I can still see Dad getting all bundled up in a down coat, gloves, and my blue knit hat with a tassel on top because, even though it was cold, it was "time for Pokey's walk." Then it was time for morning chow (which Pokey had turned into an opportunity for leftover cereal-milk and a good scratch), reading the morning paper (i.e., naptime at Dad's feet), and so on throughout the day. Eventually, when Pokey "talked" to Dad, Dad talked back. Dad took over feeding him—including people-treats that used to make him roll his eyes at us when *we* gave them to the dog. He and Pokey walked twice a day at pretty much the same pace and ended the day where they'd started—with Dad in bed and Pokey at the foot of it on the floor, making sure the old Colonel was tucked in properly.

Pokey wasn't with us for long, but it was clear that he had a purpose: to be Dad's partner—and coach—in what had been his heretofore solo retirement. Even as a kid, I could see Dad's personality change from gruff and grumbly to engaged and more energized. Don't get me wrong; he was always kind of Lone Ranger-ish. But his version of Trigger, in the package of a short, four-legged, floppy-eared dog, was what carried him into a more satisfying and less solo retirement.

A Tale of a Tail

To look at their resumés, it's hard to believe that Linda and Allen Anderson would have any time for pets. Allen is a prolific writer and photographer; Linda is an award-winning playwright, screenwriter, and fiction writer. Both teach writing classes at the Loft Literary Center in Minneapolis, and in their "spare time" they manage a very busy public-speaking schedule so they can share their expertise with their many readers, students, and fans. But ask them about their family, and their answer always includes two-legged, four-legged, and winged family members. That's just the way it's always been.

When their children grew up and moved away, Linda and Allen found themselves pondering the second halves of their lives. What did they want to do? What was going to be their contribution to the world, besides the loving, good children they'd raised? They were talking about it one day during one of their many dog-walks around the lake by their home.

The dog being walked was Taylor. She was a beautiful, happy, six-year-old Lab who drew attention everywhere she went because she always seemed to be smiling. She'd stare earnestly into the faces of every passerby, disarming them with her smile and wagging tail. Linda and Allen had always remarked on how Taylor seemed to know who needed a smile that day, because she gravitated to those who seemed stressed or preoccupied. She was like a four-legged therapist. And that's when it hit them.

Linda and Allen knew they wanted to bring more love into the universe. It's exactly what their own pets had been doing for them their entire lives. What if they could take that love and spread it through their writing, speaking, and teaching about the spiritual connections between people and animals? What if, through the power of story, they could help people understand and experience the love animals so willingly offered? Taylor smiled at them. They absolutely knew what they had to do.

And that's how the Angel Animals Network was born: a robust website and series of books and newsletters where people can share amazing stories about their pets and the love and miracles they bring into their lives. It also helps raise awareness about and support for animal rescue and adoption organizations to connect more loving pets with people who will love them back.

Which leads me to …

How to See Miracles in Your Own Pets

I sat down with Linda Anderson to find out how she and her husband help people to see the miracles pets bring us. That very question made Linda smile and take a deep breath as if to say, where should I begin? I immediately knew I'd found the expert I'd been looking for.

First, Linda says, it's important to reflect on what was going on in your life at the time your pet arrived. Most of the time, if you do a grid of your life and mark when the pet showed up, you can see that it came at exactly the right time with the right lessons or blessings you needed just then. Like at a time when you were feeling particularly abandoned or alone or frustrated; and the animal shows up with this unconditional love, this loyalty, this message that you are not alone. "Divine Messengers" is what Linda calls them: our connection to unconditional, Divine love.

So, with that setting the scene, pay attention to your pet. Besides living in a state of unconditional love, they live fully in the present. That's where the joy is. When you're starting to feel that sense of frustration—like I did on my walk with Max in thirty-below weather—pull back and look. Try to see through the animal's eyes. What are they looking at? Smelling? Noticing? It will open up a whole new world to you, one that you—stuck in your own worries and thoughts—are totally missing. Your pet is your connection and guide to that exciting world. Just get out of your own head and follow.

It's also good to think of your pet as a mirror of yourself. You are attracted to qualities in your pet that actually are qualities you admire in yourself: love, loyalty, having your priorities in the right place. On the flip side, pets also mirror what you may be lacking. Maybe you don't have as much joy or ability to live in the present as you'd like to have, but you have this animal who is an expert at it. Maybe he or she can show you how.

Finally, Linda concedes that pet ownership is not always easy. Sometimes animals come into our lives and really test us, stretching our patience and pushing us to the brink of questioning our decision to have them in the first place. But again, pull back and pay attention. It's likely that the qualities you had to call upon to accommodate that pet are exactly those you needed to develop at the time. Linda says it is amazing how many stories she hears from people who were on the brink of relinquishing their pet to an animal shelter or finding a new home for him, only to wind up treasuring that animal for the many gifts it brought them in return.

So, look at the connections, the continuum from when your pet showed up, to where you're at in your life today. Likely, your Divine Messenger has been by your side the entire time, with just the right lessons, love, and guidance. All you needed to do was pay attention.

Chapter Seven: Being Someone Else's Miracle

You Know That Movie *It's a Wonderful Life*?

It's all about how one man, George Bailey, thinks his life has been nothing but a failure and a disappointment—to his wife and kids, his community, and himself. After his dreams of traveling the world and busting out of his small town have been postponed beyond the point of realization, and having failed at the very job he postponed his dream for, he came to believe that the world would have been better had he never been born. At that point, Clarence—the angel—appeared and showed George just how successful his life had actually been—and gave him a glimpse of what the world would have been like without him.

While it can be easy to see miracles in other people's lives or to credit others with being a miracle in yours, we often don't think about the many little miracles we ourselves make happen. The stories that follow are about exactly that: people who are just being themselves, going about their daily lives, but without whom someone else's life would be missing a miracle. Read on.

"Happy Meal"

People used to make fun of my dad, the old Colonel. He'd been retired from the Marine Corps for more than twenty years, yet you could still set your watch by his militaristic schedule. At 1:00 every afternoon, his big, shiny Cadillac would come rolling down the main street of town like a tank and park outside of Konsella's Drugstore, where he'd buy the daily newspaper.

By 1:20 p.m., he'd be reading that paper in his usual booth at the Big Steer Restaurant, where he'd have his daily lunch of soup and coffee, followed by a small strawberry ice cream sundae. He'd be there exactly an hour, after which he would run the necessary errands for the household: groceries, carwash, post office, etc. By 3:15 he'd be walking into McDonald's for his afternoon cup of coffee and to read *USA Today*, which he would then bring home for my mom by 4:15, because she loved working the crossword puzzle in it.

To most people, Dad's strict schedule was an amusing quirk. But to one family on one hot day in August, it was a miracle.

Dad was walking out of McDonald's precisely at 4:00 when he saw a young mother standing outside her car, crying. She was pregnant and had three more little ones in tow; none of whom was pleased one bit about the apparent delay in their fun. He walked over and asked the young woman what was wrong. She said her car had broken down—again—and she couldn't reach her husband, and she didn't know what she was going to do. By this time, her little ones' impatience had grown to a fever pitch.

Dad pointed to the car dealer just across from McDonald's, saying he was sure that they could tow and fix her car in no time. Tearfully, the woman shook her head. She and her husband didn't have that kind of money. But she thanked Dad for his time and said she was going to go in and use the pay phone one more time to see if she could reach her husband at his job.

Dad watched the small children fall in like ducklings behind their mother as she plodded into the restaurant. He looked back at the car dealership. It was where he always bought and serviced his cars. He knew they'd have been able to take good care of her. He got into his car and left.

The young mother, still unable to reach her husband, had finally surrendered to her children's pleas and gotten them a Happy Meal to share. They emerged from McDonald's, only to find a tow truck busily hooking up the front end of her car. Frantically, she hurried over to find out what was going on.

"We're from the car dealer across the street," said the mechanic. "We're going to take your car over there and fix it."

"You don't understand," said the woman. "I told that man that I don't have any money." The mechanic smiled. "Your bill's been taken care of already."

Nearly a year later, Dad was sitting in his usual booth at McDonald's for his afternoon coffee. A brawny, worn-looking young man began walking his way. "Are you Colonel Patrow?" he asked.

The man seemed emotional—mad or sad, it was hard to tell. But Dad nodded. The man held out his hand.

"You helped my wife last summer. I wanted to thank you."

Dad stood up. There in the doorway stood the young mother, a new baby now in her arms, and the other little ones swarming around her feet. She smiled. After her car had been fixed, she'd returned to ask if anyone knew the man who'd helped her that day. She'd described him and the time of day he was there. Of course, everyone knew who it was.

As soon as her husband could get off work for an afternoon, they came to see if they could find the old Colonel. The young father had tears in his eyes as he shook Dad's hand. "I don't know what my family would have done if you hadn't been here when you were. It was a miracle."

"The Right Call"

I met my friend Jenine many years ago when I first started working with her husband Mark at the TV station. He's one of, if not *the* best, photojournalists in the country. I describe him as being able to see everything with a "child's eye": brand new and wonderful and full of possibilities, which is a rarity among seasoned (i.e., cynical) journalists. Spend a day with Mark, and you're infused with his energy and positive spirit. His wife Jenine is the same way. She walks into a room and you just feel better.

So anyway, I was talking to Mark about my book, and he said that I absolutely had to talk to Jenine about a miracle involving her sister. I called her, and sure enough, if you don't yet believe in the miracle of a well-timed phone call, here's proof.

Jenine and her older sister Marsha are very close. Even though Jenine lives here in Minnesota, and Marsha lives in Iowa, they talk at least every week and share their lives and love and support with each other.

It was Christmastime, mid-December. Jenine remembers that it was about four o'clock in the afternoon, because it was starting to get dark in Minnesota. She decided to call her sister just then. No particular reason. Maybe get some gift ideas for her kids. But when Marsha answered, it was anything but one of their normal phone calls.

Jenine pauses here to describe Marsha. "If you know Marsha, you know she's always been very sharp and witty and quick. But when she answered the phone that day, she sounded sleepy. I asked her if she'd just woken up from a nap, which would be understandable, since Marsha is a nurse and works a very early shift at the local hospital on the day-surgery unit. She mumbled something in agreement, so I just kept on with the conversation."

But as Jenine went on, Marsha didn't seem to become any more alert. In fact, she kept repeating herself. She told Jenine that she'd had a terrible headache and had gone to see the doctor, but that he'd simply sent her home to get some rest. She was scheduled for a CT scan in a couple of days, in case it didn't get better. Then she told her the same story again. And again.

Now, Jenine is a very calm person by nature. But this conversation was getting her rattled. Her own body began feeling panicky; heart racing, stomach tightening, breathing hard. She asked Marsha where her husband was, and she replied that he was at work. Marsha had told their three children that she wasn't feeling well and that she needed to rest, so they were leaving her alone. It was just what her doctor had ordered.

Jenine realized she had begun talking to Marsha like she would a three-year-old: "Okaaay … well, you just take care of yourself, now. I'll call back later to check on you, okaaay?" But the calm she tried to convey over the phone was not what she was feeling hundreds of miles away.

Jenine said that when she hung up, she burst into tears, which also was not like her. Immediately her mind raced over who she could call to go check on her sister. She tried but couldn't reach Marsha's husband at work. Their father, who also lived in Iowa, wasn't home either. He wasn't one to use his cell phone, and rarely turned it on. But when Jenine dialed his number in desperation, miraculously he picked up. He was shocked to hear his normally calm and collected daughter sobbing. He tried to calm *her* down and assure her that everything was probably all right, but that he would call Marsha just to make sure.

When he called Marsha—whether he talked to her or one of her kids, Jenine doesn't remember—the answer he got was not to his satisfaction. He could also feel that something wasn't right. So he drove over to her house immediately, saw what Jenine had heard, and immediately took Marsha to the hospital.

Marsha had been a nurse at this hospital for twenty years, so as soon as her father came in with her, one of the neurosurgeons recognized her and the fact that she was seriously impaired and immediately whisked her off for assessment, then emergency surgery.

It turned out that Marsha had a condition called *aqueductal stenosis*, something she was born with, in which the drainage ducts for the fluid around her brain were too narrow. It had taken that long into adulthood for them to stop working altogether and for fluid to build up dangerously around her brain. The intense pressure was causing her headache. The surgeon surgically implanted a shunt that would drain the fluid down into her abdomen, and she was fine.

When the surgeon came out, he told Marsha's dad that had he not gotten Marsha to the hospital when he did, she would have died. That if she had followed her other doctor's orders and just stayed home in bed to rest and sleep, it was likely she never would have woken up.

Marsha is fine now. She will have to wear a shunt for the rest of her life, but she's healthy. Jenine tells me she believes it was *Divine intervention* that she called Marsha when she did; and that their dad was reachable and nearby when he was, and that the neurosurgeon saw Marsha and reacted as quickly as he did. They were all God's instruments that day. They and the telephone.

"A Good Time for a Breakdown"

I told you how my Dad was so regimented, even after he retired from the Marine Corps, that we knew exactly where he'd be at each hour of the day? It used to make us crazy, especially Mom, since she was one of those people who couldn't be on time even if you set every clock in the house—including her watch— an hour ahead without her knowing. Somehow she'd intuit how to be at least fifteen minutes late to anything.

Anyway, I remember I was home from college one summer when my mom's car broke down. I happened to be driving it at the time, right in downtown Chippewa Falls. Not that it's a metropolis, but when you're going down the main drag and the power steering and power brakes go out, it's pretty unsettling. I muscled my way through a right-hand turn past the post office and rolled to a stop in front of The Styling Post Beauty Shop, where Mom got her hair done. Except it wasn't open that day. And the car was dead.

It was 3:15 p.m. That meant Dad was at McDonald's, right? I had enough change for one phone call (cell phones weren't around yet). So I walked down to the post office and looked up McDonald's number in the phone book. It occurred to me as I was dialing how odd it might sound that I was calling a fast food restaurant to find my father. A pleasant woman's voice answered. "Hello! McDonald's!"

"Hi. This is Kris Patrow. You don't know me, but my father—"

"Oh, you're the Colonel's daughter! Sure, honey, he's right here. Let me go get him." Like it was normal that I'd be calling him there. Not a minute later, I heard his voice.

"Hello, Kris?"

"Hi, Dad."

"Is everything all right?"

"Mom's car broke down. I'm stranded by the post office."

And in less than fifteen minutes, there was Dad, pulling around the corner in his big, shiny Cadillac. The Markquardt Motors tow truck wasn't far behind. They said I was lucky the car didn't cause an accident—some major fuel-line malfunction or something like that; I don't know. What I do know is that I never made fun of my Dad's militaristic clock-watching again. Okay, well, maybe a little. But I sure appreciated it a lot more.

"Driver's Ed"

When I was sixteen I had two big dreams. First, to get my driver's license, and second, to become a singer in a band (after I graduated high school, of course).

I was working on the first dream—driving with my Dad around the fairgrounds—when the second one came up in conversation. "So, what do think you want to do when you graduate?" he asked as I navigated his car round and round the empty lot.

"Oh, I'm going to be a singer in a band," I said matter-of-factly.

I'm sure this isn't what the father of a sixteen-year-old girl wants to hear, like, *ever*. But instead of dismissing my dream or getting angry, which would have made me want to do it even more, my Dad said something brilliant.

"Well, that's great," he said. "You're such a good singer. Of course, it will take some time to break into the business. So make sure you go to college and learn a skill so you can support yourself until you become famous."

Now that I'm a parent of two girls, I can only imagine my Dad's horror at my stated career path. But the way he reacted was priceless. He believed in me. He talked to me like a grown-up. He helped me plan how to get there. I felt validated, which was even more important to me than being a famous singer in a band. I've never forgotten that, and I treat my own children's dreams accordingly.

By the time I went to college—allegedly to learn a means to support myself until I became famous—I already had switched dreams. But because of how my dad reacted to my first dream, I never doubted I could get there.

How to Be Someone Else's Miracle

This one is tricky. None of the people in these stories set out to be someone else's miracle. None of them wore a red cape and inserted themselves into another person's crisis with the intention of saving the day.

As I was pondering this the other day, I heard an ad on my car radio. It said something like, "Remember the time you *almost* volunteered at the soup kitchen? The time you *almost* brought a meal to your neighbor who has AIDS? Remember the time you *almost* gave money to that women's shelter?" The ad went on to say that while these are all good intentions, "almost" giving is the same as not giving at all. Don't "*almost* give." *Give.*

That really hit home. I almost always have good intentions. But how many times have I acted on them?

I think being someone else's miracle is often simply a matter of paying attention to what's going on around you and how it moves you. If you see a need—like my dad did in McDonald's parking lot—and can be part of the solution, act. Maybe it's just in a small way. But your idea of "small" may be someone else's idea of a miracle.

When you get a gut feeling that you should call someone or go see someone, do it. That gut feeling might be your signal from the universe that your particular kind of red cape—be it a shoulder to cry on or some helpful advice—is exactly what's needed at the time.

Most of the time, being someone else's miracle simply means showing up and letting the situation show you how to be your own best self.

Chapter Eight: 20/20 Hindsight Miracles

These Are My Favorite.

They are hard to put your finger on, because 20/20 hindsight miracles take a little perspective, a lot of self-examination, and—the hardest part, but the best—forgiveness. It's a way of blessing your life's journey for all its taught you, good times and bad.

I was just reading Marianne Williamson's book *The Gift of Change*, in which she explains how there's a Divine plan for each of us, made lovingly by God and implemented by a loving Holy Spirit, the goal of which is to help us remember who we really are—pure love and perfect, as created by God. This plan is for our ultimate good. So, even the bad choices we make along the way and the repercussions from them can be blessed for where they lead us on this journey. Our destination is inevitable glory. So whatever gets us there, ultimately, is a miracle.

I know it's a stretch, but take it from me—someone who's made her share of mistakes along the way. Forgiving and blessing the "bad" things and "bad" people I've encountered is a whole lot happier way to live than carrying around the baggage of regret and resentment. So, if you can bear it, take a look at your bad times (maybe you're in one right now) and try to find some nugget of good that you learned from it, some way that it helped you become a better person.

If you can't get there yet, go ahead and read on.

"Join the Club"

My earliest memory is of getting hit in the head with a golf club.

I think I was about four. I remember it was one of those sticky summer nights, which—being in Wisconsin—means it was probably late July or early August. Mom and Dad and I were sitting around the table in our pink kitchen, finishing dinner. (I always have to mention our Pepto-Bismol-pink kitchen because, to this day, it's what all of my high school friends and former boyfriends remember.) The door was open so the screen door could let in any breeze that dared challenge the dead night air.

I was in a hurry to finish eating because my older brother Steve had already gone outside to "hang out," which, to his adoring little sister, was a mysterious and alluring "big kid" activity to be followed and explored. Most nights, from my point of view, it just looked like he was sitting on the curb under the streetlight with a bunch of his friends, talking—which seemed pretty boring. So I was certain that there must be something magical about it and, if I just followed them around enough, I would finally figure out what it was.

It was slow going, eating a hot dinner on a hot night. I guzzled milk with every bite. But I knew better than to complain or not clean my plate. My dad was a retired Marine colonel who demanded decorum and respect, even if it was about macaroni and cheese. My mom, on the other hand, was just content to sit and talk the night away at the kitchen table, since all of us were usually out at school, work, or playing. It was the one time of day when she was guaranteed a captive audience.

After about an eon, I asked to be excused, which the Colonel granted, since I had finished my dinner. I hurried over to the screen door but came to a screeching halt. First obstacle: I knew I needed to be very quiet so that Steve wouldn't hear me and make himself scarce to keep his little sister from tagging along. But the screen door always stuck and needed to be kicked at an exact spot on the baseboard for it to open. I wriggled my sneaker off and pointed my toes up so that the fleshy ball of my foot would make the impact and not make as much noise. *Thud.* It worked! The baseboard dislodged, and the rusty spring made a wang-wang-wang sound as it strained against the swinging door. I scurried out and held the door so it wouldn't bang as it closed. At that point, I decided to lose the other shoe too, thinking that if the Indians could walk more quietly without them, so could I.

I squinted to adjust my eyes between the glaring, bare light bulb on the back porch and the fizzling sunlight on the horizon. Off to my right, I saw Steve—not under the streetlight like he usually was but in the neighbor's yard with his back to me. (Lucky!) He was standing funny, I remember: legs apart so they made an inverted "V" with his hips. He kept toddling from one foot to the other, as if the grass was tickling his feet. He was looking down, and his shoulders were all hunched in front of him so that it looked like he didn't have arms at all.

This must be part of the hanging out ritual, I thought. And how lucky I was to catch him alone. I'd have a better chance at not being shooed away like a pesky fly. Maybe Steve would tell me what was so fascinating down on the ground and why he was doing that odd little dance. I ran as fast as I could on my tippy-toes, up behind him, careful not to disturb his trance or whatever he was staring at down below. I got close enough so that my head was level with his hips, and I began to look down too, when—

Whap!

Lights out. I don't remember being hit by Steve's golf club or being in pain or feeling the cool grass as my face apparently hit it, or my brother's voice yelling in horror for Mom and Dad. Next thing I knew, I was in my little, red corduroy housecoat that Grandma had made me, with the soft, fake, white fur around the collar and the wrists. I was sitting on Mom's lap in the car, and she had a great, big bath towel wound up on top of my head like a turban. I saw a skinny black figure shrinking in the bright porch light as Dad hit the gas down the driveway. It must be Steve, I thought, since he wasn't in the car with us. I tried to remember any glimpses of his secret ritual that I might have seen before the *thwap* happened, then ...

Lights out again.

The next time I opened my eyes, I thought I had died. All I saw was whiteness, although it looked suspiciously like a sheet over my face, and it kept moving slightly with each tug I felt on my head. I heard a man's voice that wasn't my dad's. I supposed it was God examining my head for some reason. Tug, tug, tug. I remember worrying that my brother would get in trouble for killing me and get grounded for the rest of his life, when it wasn't really his fault. Whatever he was doing that was potentially lethal for four-year-olds, he hadn't known I was there. I was wishing I could wake up long enough to tell Mom and Dad that, so Steve wouldn't hate me forever. Maybe when I'm an angel, I thought, I could just float down and tell it to them in a vision. That thought provided a little comfort. Then I began to wonder if heaven had any colors at all, because if this was what it was going to look like for all eternity, it was going to be way boring.

Then all of a sudden, I heard my mom's voice ask the God-voice a question. I couldn't quite make it out, except that I knew it was Mom. Her voice sounded all wiggly and breathy—like mine did when I was just finishing crying but couldn't stop the sobs all at once and I'd keep whimpering with big breaths in between. What was my mom doing in heaven? I mean, I knew she'd get there eventually, but Dad and Steve still needed her to make dinner for them and make sure they had clean clothes and tell them the same stories fifty million times. I was going to send her back if I had any say about it. Then, just as I was about to have a word with God—*thwoop!*

Heaven got yanked off of my head, and there was the face that went with the God-voice. He looked like an ordinary, older man with no hair on top of his head—just thready gray stuff on the sides. He had big, square glasses framed in thick, black plastic, just like my Dad's. As he looked down at me, his chin made other chins in his neck. He smiled. Well, I thought to myself, I actually thought God would be more Moses-like—like the one we saw every Easter on *The Ten Commandments*. But I guess no one really knows what God looks like till they get to heaven. At least He was smiling.

But then my Mom's face sidled in next to His, and I began thinking, if this was heaven, Mom wouldn't be crying. And God wouldn't need glasses. And it smelled in there, like when Mom scrubbed the floor with Pine Sol. I didn't think they needed to clean floors in heaven.

Through her tears, Mom smiled and said, "Everything's going to be all right." It occurred to me that I must not be dead after all. Did this mean I was going to get in trouble along with Steve, and we'd both be grounded in our bedrooms forever? (Notice how my selfless thoughts turned selfish as soon as I realized I was still Earth-bound.) Mom helped me sit up, and I saw that I was in the hospital. My legs dangled over the side of the gurney, and when I looked down I could see the towel Mom had had on my head. It was all bloody, except for the places where it had been folded, so it made kind of a neat design. God, who turned out to be some doctor named Doctor Miniquez, was telling my mom how to take care of the bump on my head and when to come back to get the stitches out.

Stitches? I reached up and felt a bump that seemed to stand out a foot beyond my head. I imagined that I looked like Wile E. Coyote after he ran off the side of the cliff and onto his head, before the Acme Ambulance Company came to scrape him up off the ground again. My fingers scrambled over my bare scalp, trying to find out what they had done with my hair around the bump. And on the top of the bump, thick snatches of thread went in one side and came out the other: stitches. That was what the tugging must have been, I thought. He was sewing my head back together. For a moment, I thought that was pretty cool, until I remembered that they had shaved my hair off to do it, and now Steve and his friends would have one more reason to tease me.

Mom gathered me up and took me out into the hall, where my Dad came walking up to us with a Styrofoam cup of coffee. Dad never liked hospitals. He couldn't stand the gory stuff, which now, as a grown-up, I think is odd, given that he fought in one of the bloodiest battles of World War II at Pelé lieu. The minute we got to the emergency room, he offered to go get Mom some coffee while they stitched me up. But when he did see me, upright and not bloody anymore, he quickly put the coffee down and gave me his big, bear-like "Dad-Hug."

Dad-Hugs were the best. Somehow he was able to curl his giant shoulders around me at the same time his arms held me tight; I could rest my forehead in that soft place between his ear and his chin; not quite his face, not quite his neck. Even when I got old enough so that my legs no longer dangled from his hugs but stood firmly on the floor beside him, no hug could match my dad's. Wherever I was, I felt swallowed up in safety and love.

They drove me home. I remember seeing Steve's skinny silhouette frozen in the glaring back porch light as we approached the house. Apparently, he hadn't moved since we'd left. I had learned on the way home that Steve had been practicing his golf swing when I sneaked up behind him, and that his club had met with my head on his backswing. He was mortified and terrified. I don't remember Mom or Dad yelling at him that night, although I'm sure they did eventually. I just remember the look on Steve's face as I passed by him in Dad's arms: his green eyes wide, his skin kind of a limey-gray, like he had just eaten something bad. Motionless and speechless, his eyes scanned me top to bottom. Then I saw fear dissolve into relief, and his shoulders, which had been hovering somewhere around his ears, dropped like someone had just cut the strings on a puppet. He hung his head and followed us into the house.

Some would characterize this first memory of mine as a bad one. I've thought about it many times—like whenever a new stylist cuts my hair and asks, what the heck happened to your head? (There's a bald dent on the top that never attempted to grow hair back.) Or when I embellish the story at family reunions and make Steve out to be the Devil—in his presence, of course, so that he can tease me back and say that I deserved it. But I've never thought of the memory as bad. First, I was on the kind of adventure that every little sister loves: getting a sneak peek into the mysterious doings of her older teenage brother. Then, I woke up in heaven. And finally, I found myself back in my parents' loving arms, safe and sound—not to mention that Steve waited on me hand and foot for months after that with love and kindness that he denies to this day.

But I'll always (fondly) remember. And besides, after that, Steve let me tag along whenever I wanted to, which was the whole point of my adventure in the first place.

"Why *Not* Me?"

Ask Kristine Greer if she ever asks, "Why *me?* Why did *I* have to get cancer?" and she'll answer, "Why *not* me?"

Granted, no one ever wants cancer. No one ever gets the diagnosis and says, "Well, this could be a great experience." But nearly ten years out from that fateful day when her doctor gave her a 20-percent chance to live, Kristine counts it as a blessing.

The background: Kristine, a preschool teacher, wife, and mother of two, was no stranger to health problems. In 1993 she was diagnosed with *mastocytosis*, a rare condition in which the body produces too many *mast cells*, the cells that naturally exist to protect us from disease. With this condition, the mast cells do not respond properly to any number of triggers, ranging from stress to anesthesia to food, smells, and changes in temperature. Although doctors gave her only five years to live, Kristine learned to avoid her triggers, lead a healthy lifestyle, and manage her disease. It was in keeping with that plan that she went in for her annual physical in May 2001.

When her doctor could not find her right ovary during the normal exam, she ordered a transvaginal ultrasound and found what she believed to be a fluid-filled, grapefruit-sized cyst. She told Kristine not to worry and to come back in another month for a follow-up.

But Kristine did worry. During those thirty days she could feel her body changing. Her shorts were getting tighter, even though she was eating and exercising just the same. When she went back, the cyst had grown into the size of a football. The doctor said she didn't think it was ovarian cancer—Kristine was too young for that—but they should do some blood work just in case and schedule surgery to remove the cyst.

Most people would jump at the chance to have any potentially cancerous object removed from their bodies. But the decision wasn't so easy for Kristine. Her mastocytosis made it unsafe for her to have general anesthesia. Any surgery would have to be performed under local anesthesia like a spinal block, which meant she would be awake for the entire procedure. And once out of surgery, she couldn't have anything stronger than Tylenol for pain.

But when the blood tests came back positive for ovarian cancer, Kristine went ahead with the surgery. She watched as the surgeon removed a huge, black mass from her abdomen. She watched as the surgeon exchanged shocked glances with the anesthesiologist. She consented—with her surgeon's hands embedded in her body—to having a colorectal specialist examine her other organs to see whether the cancer had spread, all the while thinking, "Am I going to die?"

The short answer, according to her doctor, was yes. Kristine remembers the moment clearly. Her doctor's dress. Her doctor's shoes. The time on the clock. "You're stage three," she said. Immediately Kristine asked where she should go for the best treatment. Where would the doctor send her own mother?

Her doctor responded, "Let me tell you your odds: 20 percent." Kristine began to sob. Her husband sobbed. She asked to go home. When the doctor argued against it, Kristine said, "You told me I'm going to die. I'm going home right now."

Kristine says that the next twenty-four hours were surreal. Stripped of all hope, she tried to wrap her mind around what needed to be done before she died. Who would take care of her husband and kids? What should she do with the new clothes she had just bought but would likely never wear? Nothing made sense. She couldn't eat, couldn't sleep. And then a call came that brought her to her senses—with a sense of hope.

It was her doctor. She had sent a sample of Kristine's tumor to the Mayo Clinic for further tests. Yes, it was still cancer. But it was a rare kind, with a slightly higher chance of survival. Kristine remembers hanging up the phone, sobbing and saying to her husband, "I am gonna live. Just *watch* me!"

That small piece of hope was all Kristine needed to change from preparing for death to preparing for life. She met with the Mayo experts who, unlike her original doctor, focused on her strength and survival instincts. Because of her mastocytosis, they worried that traditional chemotherapy would be too toxic for her system. So they devised a novel treatment approach that, among other things, required significant daily doses of healthy living, stress reduction, and positive attitude. In her words, "I had my work cut out for me, and I knew it. And I was going to give it my best shot."

Kristine went home with a to-do list that covered everything from eating as healthy and organically as she could to getting rid of all the toxic chemicals in and around her home. She stopped watching TV news and started watching funny movies. While she was already blessed with great people in her life, she made sure to put a healthy distance between herself and any "glass-half-empty" types while she healed, and she directed the rest to talk only about positive things in her presence. "My goal was to surround myself with peaceful, loving energy. It was also helpful to try and let go of worrying what others thought. I've always been a peacemaker, and I didn't want anyone mad, ever! I chose a path of peace and light and meditation, and I believe it played a role in my survival."

Kristine recalls with amazement what a difference these seemingly small changes made in her life. While she had been very happy and content before, she now felt empowered and part of an even greater plan for her life. She started her own wellness company called "Green Kristine" to be a resource for others looking to make positive changes to their environment. She also founded "Charlene's Light," a foundation dedicated to educating women and the community about symptoms of ovarian cancer, raising money for ovarian cancer research, and providing support and hope for patients and families. She told me, "Until I had cancer, I could never imagine myself getting up in front of people to speak about anything. Then one morning after I returned from Mayo, I woke up with a vision of myself standing up at a podium, helping other people with cancer. I haven't been afraid since."

Once a semester, Kristine also goes to the University of Minnesota and speaks to medical students about her journey. Her message focuses on the importance of hope. "When you sit down and tell patients that they have cancer, you hold so much power in your hands. Connect with them, hold their hands and tell them you're a team and that together you will do all you can, that there's always hope and you believe in them. There is no such thing as false hope."

She's had to practice what she preaches. Every few months, Kristine returns to Mayo for follow-up tests to see if her "cancer count" is up. Sometimes it is. Then she knows she has to turn up the positive energy, reduce her stress, and focus on helping her body stay well. And then she gets those e-mails and calls from women she's helped as a result of her own experience—women who previously had ignored their vague symptoms; women who had been told by their doctors not to worry but took Kristine's advice and *did* seek more help; women who subsequently found out that they had ovarian cancer but caught it early enough to survive. And that's when she knows she's doing what she was meant to do. She and I agreed that "sometimes your purpose chooses you."

So, no, Kristine never asks, "Why me?" Instead, she says, "Why *not* me? You know, it's got to be somebody; and you've just got to say, All right, what am I going to do with this? I have to turn it around and do something." And she has.

"Mother Figure"

It was about 1:30 in the afternoon. I was sitting in Mrs. Armstrong's fifth-grade class, wondering what the evil little girl behind me was going to do to me next. Earlier that week she had poured pencil shavings down my back, which are itchier than the aftermath of any haircut you've ever had—especially when you have to leave them there and pretend nothing happened so that the other kids won't notice and laugh. And this latest prank wasn't long after she *had* caught the other kids' attention at my expense by snapping the back of my bra (make that my "training bra") so hard that it smacked my skin like a fat rubber band and made me cry. But of course I deserved all this, according to her and the rest of the popular kids, because I was fat. To get my mind off of my next inevitable attack, I imagined sitting on her head so that it looked like Wile E. Coyote when he ran headlong into a wall while trying to catch the Roadrunner—flat as a pancake.

It was easy to tune out Mrs. Armstrong, because she had a voice like Charlie Brown's teacher that just went on and on and on. The only time my ears ever perked up was when the droning stopped, because it so rarely did.

The droning stopped.

When I turned my eyes from their daze back to reality, I saw my older brother Mike standing in the doorway to our classroom. I mean my *way* older brother Mike, older by seventeen years. Like the rest of the class, I gave no visible sign of recognition because he didn't even live in Chippewa Falls. He was a Marine stationed in California. Mom and Dad never mentioned that he'd be coming home, which was usually a big deal and required lots of cleaning and food preparation at least a week in advance. But as he spoke softly to Mrs. Armstrong, she looked right at me, and then asked me to come to the front of the class. Mike put his hand on my shoulder and simply said, "We need to go home."

Home was a block and a half away—not even *that* far if you cut through the alley. Mike would only tell me that he'd come home to help Mom and that she told him to come walk me home from school.

When I got home, Mom was sitting at the kitchen table with a cup of coffee untouched in front of her. She had cupped her hands over her cheeks. In one hand dangled a twisted, what seemed to be soggy, Kleenex. But instead of throwing it away, her fingers just kept worrying it, round and around, occasionally dabbing the very tip of her nose. She sniffed and said, "Hi, honey."

"What's wrong?" Like any kid, I was mortified whenever my mom cried. Moms weren't supposed to cry. Kids were. And then moms made it all better.

Her next words didn't quite sink in, because I was so blindsided by her cried-out face. I'd never seen it before. It was all pink and puffy and wet. But I made out a phrase that sounded like, "Your dad has left."

Somehow I made it from the kitchen door to her side. I put my hand on her shoulder, the only thing I could think of in order to make her stop crying.

"What do you mean, he left?" Dad had gone to the hospital a couple of times in the middle of the night, once after falling down and another time because they thought he'd had a mild stroke. But Mom had never said that he'd *left*.

"I kicked him out."

I snatched my hand away. "What? Why?" My fifth-grade mind ran to the fact that he too was fat, and maybe Mom decided that she didn't like fat people, either.

"Because of his drinking." Mom went on to explain that Dad drank too much, that it wasn't normal for dads to fall asleep or pass out in their chairs by 8:00 every night, and that those hospital visits weren't just because he fell down or randomly suffered a mild stroke. They all had to do with his drinking. Mom had issued him an ultimatum: get sober or get out. So Dad had left.

It really was too much to take in. I didn't know that Dad wasn't "normal," that his falling asleep was due to anything other than a hard day at work every day, that he regularly drank until he could barely walk, and that it was so bad that his life was in danger. I didn't want to know. I wanted Mom to take it back. I wanted Mom to take *Dad* back.

"How could you!" I was mad. "You made him leave! Where's he going to go? When is he going to come back? Why don't you *help* him instead of just kicking him out?" I was crying now. The only other thing I remember is Mike saying that the reason he flew home and came to get me at school was because Mom was afraid that Dad would show up and take me with him.

Now, even thirty-plus years later, it's hard to write this. I can still see my mom cringing at each word I yelled at her, blinking hard like she was using her eyelids as shields. I remember storming out of the kitchen to—I don't remember where—just someplace where I could reassess my world and wonder what was going to happen to us. My brothers were both grown up and had moved away. It would be just me and Mom. And as hateful as it sounds, I never liked my mom that much or felt close to her like I did with Dad. I hated her kowtowing to him and thought that she was stupid and couldn't possibly handle all the bills and the upkeep on the house and yard and the car. I imagined all the comforts of home just tumbling down around us because Mom didn't know how to do anything. Why couldn't *she* be the one who had left?

My memory fades to black at this point, maybe because that's how it felt to me. I do remember Dad calling me, just me, telling me that he didn't know where he was going to go but that he loved me, and that maybe he would move in with Grandma. He didn't tell me it was all going to be okay. He didn't tell me when he would call again. He didn't say that he'd come home. He just left the conversation all dangling like a frayed rope—no knot, no closure to cling to. Then I was mad at *him*.

The particulars of Mom's and my daily lives after that are fuzzy. I went back to school as soon as Mom was sure that Dad wasn't going to kidnap me. Mom kept working at the library. And remarkably, dinner was still on the table every night at 6:00. The car didn't stop running. And the house didn't fall down. In fact, on more than one occasion I saw Mom dig out Dad's tools and fix whatever needed fixing: the air conditioner when it went on the fritz, the kitchen sink when it got plugged up, the lamp when its wiring fizzled, the window when its frame warped and it wouldn't slide up and down anymore. Yes, there was Marge—sometimes still wearing her skirt and nice work shoes—picking up tools like she'd done it her whole life and fixing whatever was broken. She never let regular car maintenance slip by. And once a month, she sat down at the dining room table and paid all the bills.

This may not sound like a big deal, but to me, it was. I had never thought Mom knew how to do any of this stuff. I'd thought she was dumb, when really the deal was that she and Dad had divided the chores when they got married: she was in charge of cooking, cleaning, and the kids, and he was in charge of bills, car, and house repairs. It wasn't that Mom didn't know how to do them. That's just how they divided the work. . And to tell you the truth, she was better at the repair jobs than Dad ever was. She looked as comfortable with a hammer as she did with a spatula. During that year and a half that Dad was gone, I gained a new respect for my mom. I marveled at how smart she was, how courageous, how strong. I was proud to be her daughter. I was proud of how she and I were making it on our own.

Then one day I came home from school, and there was Dad, sitting in his La-Z-Boy like he'd never left—except that there was no drink in his hand. "Hi, Poopchin!" he said, like he always did. I felt like I was in a time warp, just like when he'd left—no warning, no conversation about what was going to happen. He was just there. Mom never said a word about what had transpired, and there was no family meeting as to how things were going to be different. In fact, except for the drinking, things weren't different. Mom gladly relinquished the tools and bill-paying to Dad, although she would finesse his attempts at repairing things when he wasn't looking. Dad simply added AA meetings to his weekly routine. That was all. And after all of that, I remember feeling kind of sad that Mom's and my solo adventure was over. I liked being her partner. Without Dad, she needed me. Without Dad, like it or not, I got close to my mom, and by the time he came back, I liked that closeness and didn't want to lose it.

Years later, I found out from my brothers—not my parents—that Dad had finally gone to an alcohol treatment center to dry out, then to his mom's house (my grandma's) for a year afterward so that Mom would be convinced that he could stay sober.

I write all this because, as I look back on it now, I see this very trying time in my life as a miracle. If Mom hadn't kicked Dad out, I never would have known her or gotten close to her in the way I had to when it was just she and I. I never would have known the brave woman who chose being alone rather than being the wife of an alcoholic, the woman who chose to protect me rather than the image we had of the perfect family. I'd never wish the struggle of alcoholism on any family, don't get me wrong. But for me, the struggle produced a miracle. And for that, I will always be grateful.

"The Job Not Taken"

Remember Marti Erickson, the parenting expert who shared her expertise for "Seeing Miracles as a Parent?" Well, in the course of my discussions with her, her own 20/20 hindsight miracle came to light.

It happened when she was thirty-nine. Marti was a full-time everything: wife, mother of two, and accomplished researcher and university lecturer who had just completed her PhD. She had impressed her professors to the point where they had written a job description with her in mind, envisioning that she would join them at the University of Minnesota in a coveted, tenure-track professorship that most new PhD's would jump at. If she just hung in there—through the flurry of late nights at the library, the meticulously-referenced writing, and the hours at the typewriter and copy machine—her very predictable, secure, and profitable career path would be set.

She set her sights on this job that was so well-matched to her strengths and didn't question it; she didn't have time. Until one day she was overcome with unbearable pain in her abdomen. She rushed to the doctor, and within hours, her life changed from having and doing it all … to having cancer. There was a tumor the size of a grapefruit growing on her ovary. She had to have surgery right away. She had to deal with an uncertain prognosis and the question of how to help her two young children understand what had happened so suddenly to their healthy mom. She had to rest. Basically, cancer had handed her a forced time-out from life as she knew it, and according to Marti, it forced her to realize that "life as she knew it" wasn't the life she wanted after all.

Marti loved her family, loved working in the community and going where she was needed, loved helping people on the front lines apply the best research-based information to solving the serious problems so many children and families face. Her pre-set academic career path wouldn't allow her the flexibility to do the things she loved most. She'd have to publish according to a predetermined schedule. She'd have to be employed full-time. She'd have to rise through the ranks through the expected process. It's what everybody did.

Marti credits her cancer with helping her find her own voice, the one that said "No thank you" to the amazing job offer and instead came up with a grant proposal that allowed her to create the job she *did* want, which—when faced with losing their stellar student altogether—her professors were glad to accept.

And thus began the amazing career path Marti still finds herself on today, even three years after retiring from the university. She's traveled the world, helping communities build stronger families and helping families raise their children. She's worked as an advisor to the White House. She's shared her academic knowledge and personal insight through sixteen years of radio and TV appearances. And most of all, her untraditional, flexible career has allowed her to be the wife and mother (and now grandmother) she always wanted to be.

Cancer, Marti believes, saved her life—the life she was meant to live.

"Homecoming from Hell"

I can't believe I ever dated again after this guy.

"John" was a big, gruff, ogre kind of a guy who never quite looked entirely clean. But he was a senior and captain of the high school football team and inexplicably popular. So when he asked me, an obscure sophomore, to the homecoming dance, I succumbed to peer pressure and said yes.

At the dance, we simply sat at a table in the gym. Not much for conversation, John turned his attention to the table centerpieces made of fall leaves, pinecones, and twigs. Amidst howls of laughter by his football buddies, he proceeded to eat the centerpiece, pinecones and all.

We never danced.

But he was taking me to the nicest restaurant in town for dinner, so I still had some hope. We went in his dad's pickup, not unusual for a small town in Wisconsin. It was very clean but still had that vague manure smell wafting inside.

At the restaurant, John ordered the biggest steak available. When it came, draped over both ends of the plate, he promptly placed one elbow on either side of it, picked up the steak with his fingers, tore a chunk off, with fat, and chucked it in his mouth. My mouth fell open and stayed there for the entire dinner as he proceeded to eat his steak like a hamburger.

When he saw my steak go untouched, he wiped his mouth on his sleeve and said, "Ya gonna eat that?" I shook my head. He reached over the table, picked up *my* steak, and ate it with his fingers too.

You'd think leaving would be the end of it. But it was raining cats and dogs, so John offered to go get the truck and bring it around. I was waiting underneath the canopy when John pulled up, about six feet away. I waited for him to come around and open the door. He just sat there. I waited. He sat. Finally, he rolled down the passenger-side window and yelled, "Whatcha waiting for? Hop in!" He never understood why I wouldn't go out with him again.

The lesson here—if not a miracle—is that I learned as a teenager that just because someone is popular doesn't automatically mean they're people I have to like or be friends with. I learned that I needed to look deeper, beyond the veneer of what other people think is cool, and decide for myself whether they have the qualities that make them good relationship material for *me*. That lesson alone has saved me a lot of grief over the years, along with a lot of bad steak dinners.

"Living for Two"

My good friend Tom doesn't believe in miracles. So, out of respect for him, I'll call his story what he calls it: an extreme coincidence.

I'll start his story at the end. Tom lives the kind of life that you think exists only in the movies—Indiana Jones-type movies, that is. He is a pilot and a certified scuba instructor; he's been skydiving, flown with the Blue Angels, and routinely travels the world. My friend Sharon and I joke that whenever we can't reach him, which is often, he's probably out learning Latin or practicing metallurgy in his basement. He has done—and continues to try to do—just about everything.

The miracle (or, excuse me, extreme coincidence) is in *why* he does so.

I met Tom when I was working as a reporter at KARE 11 News in Minneapolis. He was a news photographer, and we usually worked weekends together. We spent many a Saturday chasing down criminals and parades. Sometimes criminals *at* parades. Anything goes on a Saturday, and you get to know your photographer very well on the many long car rides to and from stories.

Not long after we started working together, I noticed that Tom had an enormous vein on his left arm. It looked like an octopus had left one of its tentacles there, all raised up and angle-y. So I asked Tom what the deal was with that. He said it was from the dialysis he used to have before he got a kidney transplant.

The story goes that when Tom was seven years old, he was diagnosed with a condition known as *renal reflux neuropathy*, which basically means that the tubes between your kidneys and your bladder aren't fully formed. As a result, urine backflows from your bladder back into your kidneys and causes infections from time to time. Most people who have it never know it, because their bodies adjust to the problem as they grow older. But in Tom's case, the condition caused so much scarring on his kidneys that by the time he was twenty-five, his kidneys were failing. Only dialysis or a transplant would keep Tom alive.

Now, Tom's professional dream was to be a television news photographer, so hours of dialysis three times a week wasn't going to cut it for the long-term. His personal dream was to marry the love of his life, Brenda. But he didn't want to do that until he had a job. So he put "transplant" at the top of his dream list and decided to wait, with dialysis needles making regular appearances in his arm until then. A donor would come. He knew it. If he waited, it would come.

Now, Tom's brothers were the most likely candidates. They could donate one of their kidneys and survive on their remaining ones just fine. But Tom refused to let them even be tested. Somehow, he felt in his gut that it wasn't right. Again, he felt that if he waited, the right donor would come.

Then, early one morning at 3:30, the call came; there was a perfect match from a young man eleven years younger than Tom who had died in a car crash. This was it. Tom went to the hospital where, in a matter of hours, the kidney of the young man who had died would be keeping Tom alive.

Dream number one: check.

Dream number two fell into place as soon as Tom was able to be up and about, as news photographers have to be. He got a job shooting and editing documentaries at the PBS station in Duluth, Minnesota. And as soon as he got that job and saved enough money to buy a ring, he went on to dream number three, marrying Brenda.

You'd think the story ends there, but it doesn't. Tom went on to do all of those things I talked about at the beginning … because of the young man who had died. As he told the young man's mother in a letter, "I'm trying to live the kind of life your son may have wanted to live. I'm living for two people."

When KARE 11, one of the best—if not *the* best—photojournalist stations in the country offered him the morning photographer job. It was a promotion from weekends, except that you have to get up at 3:30 a.m., and he accepted it immediately. You'd think he'd have second thoughts about getting up at such an ungodly hour, but in all the time I've known Tom, he hasn't complained about it once. Why? Remember when he got the call that a kidney had become available? It came at 3:30 in the morning. He knew that time of day was particularly precious in his life. He says, "In my tenth-anniversary letter to the donor's family, I noted that I wake up about that same time each weekday to go to work at the job I would never have been able to do before the transplant." He told the young man's mother that he's glad to get up at that hour simply because he *can*—and all because of her son.

Had Tom taken one of his brothers' kidneys, he says, he may not have taken the rest of his life so seriously, making sure he lived it to the fullest as if someone else's dream depended on it too. Today, he is one of the most fulfilled, humble people I know. All because he refused one act of generosity to wait for what he knew was right. It was an "extreme coincidence" that allowed him to live a life of generosity in return.

"Hearing Aids"

It's not always easy seeing miracles, even when you're writing a book about it.

It was about six years ago, and I was going for a follow-up visit at the doctor's office. I had a double ear infection that just would not go away, despite two rounds of antibiotics and getting tubes put in my ears (so I could fly for my job). I hadn't been able to hear well for about two months. I finally felt better, but my hearing hadn't returned. I was thinking that the doc would say it was simply a matter of time and send me on my way with some ear drops and a little reassurance.

He didn't.

He walked into the exam room, took a quick look in each ear, and said, "Well, there's nothing else we can do. You've got permanent hearing loss. Come back in two weeks and I'll fit you for hearing aids." (His bedside manner was a little lacking.)

What? I'm only forty-one. I had an *earache*. Now you're saying I'm permanently deaf?

He must have thought that the incredulous look on my face was due to not hearing very well. So he simply said the same thing again, only louder. (Again, bad bedside manner.)

I couldn't breathe. I couldn't say anything. I wasn't ready for this. I wanted to run out of his office and burst into tears. As it was, I simply did my best fitness-walk sprint through the lobby, biting my lower lip so hard that I couldn't cry, and then lost it out in the hall—and all the way to my car, where I called my husband and cried even harder.

Now, the logical, calm voice in my head (to which I've given a British accent, I don't know why) said, "That doctor's an ahhhsss. We'll simply get another opinion." While the panicked, child-voice screamed above it, hyperventilating, "Oh, my God! Oh, my God! What am I gonna do? I can't hear the phone ring. I can't hear my babies cry. I can't watch TV with everyone else because I'll blow them out of the room. I can't sing because I can't hear myself ..." and on and on and on. Shock became fear, which became anger, which became depression. I drove home with that hot-eyed, dry-throat feeling you get after you've cried all the tears and snot out of your head, but you still feel like crap and that the world as you knew it twenty minutes ago has ended.

Okay, a little dramatic, I know; but twelve miles is a long way to drive when scenes from the movie *The Miracle Worker* (ironic, huh?) keep flashing through your mind and you're wondering whether you could ever learn how to spell W-A-T-E-R with your hands, much less read the lips of a two-year-old who couldn't pronounce her r's or l's yet.

When I pulled into the driveway, Dave rushed out with a hug and the number to the Mayo Clinic. I used it to schedule an appointment for their first opening, which was in three weeks. My plans to write about miracles that day kind of went down the toilet. To tell you the truth, I felt kind of betrayed. And mocked. Like God and the universe were saying, "Okay, little Miss I-See-Miracles. See the miracle in *this*."

I do pray every night, even on days like this. For me, saying thanks for all the things that are *right* with my life makes me feel better and keeps things in perspective. For example, not being able to hear was providing me with uninterrupted sleep, despite an eight-month-old and two-year-old sleeping (and often, *not* sleeping) across the hall. So I told God I was willing to consider the possibility that something good was going to come out of this. I had no idea what, but I was open to the idea. Amen.

The next morning my eyes were still puffy from my marathon crying session. And I had that crying headache that makes me want to eat McDonald's like I did in college after a night of drinking. I told Dave I'd settle for a Starbucks after we dropped the girls off at daycare. If I was going to be deaf, I'd at least have to be extra alert; and an unreasonably expensive Venti-nonfat-Chai latte was the way to go.

So I'm walking into Starbucks, and I open the door, and there's this big sign on an easel in the entryway. It has a big picture of some mint-green, frozen, coffee-thing on it, and all it says, in big letters, is:

"Why can't a quiet moment be an adventure?"

I stopped so fast that Dave walked right into me. Why can't a *quiet* moment be an adventure?

I didn't say anything at the time. I honestly thought I might have misread the sign. So I went back the next day, not necessarily wanting the coffee, but wanting to make sure I had read the sign correctly.

It was still there, exactly as I had read it the morning before.

Three weeks later, I was in the waiting area at Mayo Clinic before my appointment, and I picked up Marianne Williamson's book *The Gift of Change*. The particular chapter I was reading was all about how to remain miracle-minded in the face of life's problems. *Ding ding ding ding*. I felt a big, whopping "*Duh!*" come out of my head, and I ate a little humble pie for being so pissed off at God that day weeks before. He was preparing me for something. Now, years later, with most of my hearing restored without hearing aids, thank you very much, I've got some perspective on the gift that experience was.

Losing part of one of my senses made me pay attention to using all of them more. I noticed things: sights, smells, touches, (loud) sounds.

I appreciated them more. I appreciated and had greater patience for people who had disabilities. I no longer got angry with my mom for not hearing and having to have the TV so loud that the neighbors could hear it. I became ... a better person.

So I guess what I'm saying is, yeah ... it can be hard seeing and hearing life's miracles sometimes. I still struggle to hear during meetings and in loud social situations, and I still get frustrated sometimes with others. But at least I'm more aware of the many silent miracles that can be going on all around me if I just pay attention. God told me that a quiet moment could be an adventure. He's been right.

"Bowling for Dollars"

You could call Ed Karwinski a lot of things: "Lefty," since he bowls with his left hand; "anti-social," since he refuses to talk, drink beer, or high-five during a game; or "champ," since his unorthodox approach to bowling, both physically and socially, has resulted in more than fifty 300-games and more than twenty-five 800-series.

One of the last things you'd probably ever think to call Ed is "disabled." But technically, he is. Ed Karwinski was born with cerebral palsy.

Ed was about two years old when his parents realized that something wasn't right. Ed was taking too long to learn how to walk. He kept trying but kept falling down. Doctors soon diagnosed him with cerebral palsy, an injury to the brain that likely occurred during pregnancy or delivery. It affected Ed's right side. But he credits his family with never letting it affect the way they treated him or what they expected from him.

If little Eddie couldn't keep up with his six siblings during the Michigan winters, his sisters would simply put him on one of those round plastic saucers they used for sledding and just drag him along. "Eddie the Omelet" they called him. In the summer, they'd take him to baseball games and have him squeeze a baseball over and over again to strengthen his arm. He fell in love with the game, so when he wanted to try out, they encouraged him to go for it. Even though he did everything left-handed, he played well enough to become a pitcher for his Little League team.

Despite his love for baseball, Ed knew that with his right side the way it was, baseball wasn't a long-term option for him beyond the summer pony leagues in his hometown. But he loved competition, so when he graduated from high school, he started hanging around with his buddies at the local bowling alley, thinking that a one-handed sport was something he probably could do. He admits he was a little reluctant; he'd had a bad experience with kids teasing him when he tried to bowl during junior high. Besides, all of the bowling balls were right-handed, which he was not. So his game, in his words, "stunk." Then one day while he was hanging out, he saw Dan Bush, the manager of the bowling alley and one of the premier bowlers in the Detroit area, throw one of his old balls away. Ed was intrigued. Dan was a lefty just like he was. So Ed went over and dug the ball out of the trash, and it fit him like a glove. And it rolled down the alley like it had eyes. It, Ed says, was a miracle.

Ed got himself a job at the bowling alley so he could practice for free and get pointers from Dan. He practiced during the week, and every Saturday his mom would drop him off at the alley at 9:00 a.m., and he would bowl until she picked him back up at 3:00. He entered a tournament and won. He entered the next one and won again. He began making money. In 1988, he started playing in a Detroit area league and made quite the impression for a rookie, bowling six 300 games and four 800 series, and winning a tournament in Las Vegas. He literally was bowling for—and winning lots of—dollars.

Ed's bowling career to date reads like any serious bowler's dream. He bowls in as many leagues and tournaments as his schedule and wallet will allow, amassing 200+ averages and victories that have become too numerous to count. He has played national tournaments when he could afford to go, but he prefers to stay within driving distance of any competition to keep his "hobby" profitable.

All the time he was telling me his story, Ed never once sounded resentful about being born with a disability—even when he told me about being teased or being left out because of it. When I asked him whether he'd ever said "Why me?," this is what he said.

"Here's somebody who grabs a bowling ball out of the garbage, and it lights up his life. If things had been different, if I hadn't taken that old, left-handed ball out of the garbage, I never would have known this miracle that has become my life. I see so many other kids who are worse off than I ever was, and I get tears in my eyes. I pray: Lord, if you're going to put somebody into this situation, give them an out, like you did for me."

Give them their own magic "bowling ball."

Afterword

Pay it Forward

I just saw this movie again recently. *Pay It Forward* is about a little kid who takes his assignment in social studies class very seriously. The assignment? To change the world. The boy's idea is to help as many people as he can, asking only that they "pay it forward" to someone else in return. This way, the miracles multiply exponentially.

I had the same experience in news when I was an intern. Despite my lack of skill and lowly status, the star anchor of the sports department, John Maino, offered to help me put my first resume tape together. I was so bad and so green, this was certainly a challenge. But he sat with me for hours, painstakingly making me look so much better on tape than I actually was. I was humbled by his help but had no means of repaying him.

"How can I ever repay you?" I asked at about 3:30 that morning as he handed me my stellar tape.

"Just do the same thing for someone else who deserves it," he said. "Just pass it on." And that's how I leave this chapter and my book, asking readers—whatever they've gotten from this book, even if it's only a laugh—to "Pay it Forward." That in itself will be the best miracle of all.

Conclusion

How to See Miracles in Your Own Life

The beauty beyond the storm.
There's a beautiful picture where ever you are. You just need
to find it.

Often, when we were out on news stories, the assignment editor would call us up and ask us to "get a weather shot." You know, that pretty video that meteorologists use for their background during their weather forecasts? Well, that comes from a news photographer who's out on some unrelated assignment and is charged with bringing back something beautiful for viewers to look at for thirty seconds or so. That may not sound hard to do, but those assignment editors always seemed to call when we'd be driving along some empty highway during a drought

149

or leaving a story on bad landlords in a dilapidated neighborhood. You don't have time to drive to a park. You have to find something beautiful *there—now.*

It's kind of the same thing with learning how to see miracles in your own life. No matter where you are, no matter what situation you're in, you have to find your "weather shot"—something beautiful about where you are, right now.

Look. Listen. Wait if you have to. If you believe in them, they will come.

Maybe it's the sunbeam that comes streaming through your (dirty) kitchen window just when you're feeling low.

Maybe it's your long-lost best friend from high school calling with some encouragement or advice right when you need it.

Maybe you'll hit all the green lights on the very day you thought you'd be late for work. Say thank you. This is the universe or God—or whatever you call the good energy in this existence—sending you your own personal miracles. All you have to do … is pay attention.

It's kind of like the movie *Field of Dreams* with Kevin Costner. The mantra is this: "If you build it, he will come." In my experience, it's the same way with miracles. If you believe in them, they will come.

About the Author

Ask Kris Patrow to describe herself and she'll say, "I am a reporter of miracles." Her many years as an award-winning television news reporter inspired her to begin writing this ultimate "newscast"—one filled with behind-the-scenes miracles that never made the air, and daily miracles we're all witness to but have forgotten how to "see." She hopes this and future "newscasts" will help people remember how to see and experience the many miracles in their own lives.

In addition to her awards as a news reporter, Patrow has won national and regional accolades as a public relations professional. One of her proudest moments was that of getting her client—No Name® Premium Meats and Seafood of St. Michael, Minnesota—mentioned on *Late Night with Conan O'Brien* by having his likeness carved out of white chocolate with No Name Bacon for hair.

In 2001, Patrow married her soul mate, fellow newshound and miracle-seer, photographer Dave Ogle. They have three children—Dave's son Ryan and their daughters, Sam and Alex—and one crazy cat named Cookie, each of whom inspires her to keep looking for and writing about miracles in the every day.

Acknowledgments

Writing acknowledgments is nothing short of intimidating, when you consider that this book was born out of forty-seven years of inspiration, hardship, experience, and the generosity of countless people, many of whom aren't even aware of the impact they've had on my life. To all of you who have crossed my path, and to those of you who have given me the gift of your time and attention in writing this book: thank you, thank you, thank you with all of my heart.

Thank you to my exceptional, loving husband, Dave, who has believed in me—and the book in me—all of these years. Without his unwavering encouragement and support, my book would still be a collection of reporter notebooks, napkins, journal pages and dreams, lying unrealized in the countless drawers and closets throughout our home. Thanks to my angel-children: Ryan, Samantha and Alexandra, each of whom challenged and inspired me to keep seeing miracles, even when I was on my last nerve and more tired than I ever imagined was humanly possible. Thanks to my angel-dog, Max, who was always by my side, teaching me how to see miracles through the hardest years of my life. Thanks to my second-grade teacher, Miss Brunner, who said she wouldn't die until I'd published my first book. Sorry it took me so long! Thanks to my dad, the Colonel, who never expected less of me because I was a girl and who told me I could do anything I put my mind to. You were right.

Thanks to my best girlfriend of all time, Sharon. You were the first person to know the real me—and love me anyway! For more than twenty years, you have shared every smile, tear, victory, and failure with me; and it's all been worth it because of you. I love you more than you could ever know.

To the many people who unwittingly inspired me by their selfless acts of kindness during my countless "bad news" stories, thank you. To those of you who agreed to be interviewed by me for this book—Joe Bailey, Marti Erickson, Gaye Lindfors, Linda Anderson, Kristine Greer, Ed Karwinski, Jim Gehrz, Sharon, Denise, Lorri B. and Misty and Jenine—your very presence in this book makes it so much richer, so much more miraculous. Thank you.

Professor Fritzell, you were right—in so many ways. Thank you for making me a better thinker, a better writer, and a better person.

To my brothers Steve and Mike: you'll never realize how much of an influence you have had (and continue to have) on your little sister's life, how much I admire you, and how much your presence in my life means to this day. Thank you.

I also have to thank the three most amazing leaders I've ever had the privilege of working for: Kathy Tunheim, Scott Libin, and Jeff Bohnson. Your leadership by example, your encouragement and challenge to grow and become more than I ever dreamed possible, are gifts I can never repay. I only hope I can make you proud by the legacy I create in your wake.

And finally, to my mom, Marge, who died on New Year's Day this year because you wouldn't have dreamed of ruining your children's Christmas or New Year's Eve: Mom, I finally did it. You always told me I could. I promised you on your death bed that I would. The money you left to me, Mom … I used it to publish this book. I thought you'd want it that way. I love you.

Resources

Joseph Bailey, MA, LP
Author and psychologist
Speaking, counseling, and consulting
website: www.joebaileyandassociates.com
www.flyfishingseminars.com
E-mail: hrcbailey@comcast.net
Author of the following books:
> *Fearproof Your Life: How to Thrive in a World Addicted to Fear*
> Conari Press
> *Slowing Down to the Speed of Love: How to Create a Deeper, More Fulfilling Relationship in a Hurried World*
> McGraw-Hill Publishers
> *The Speed Trap: How to Avoid the Frenzy of the Fast Lane*
> Harper San Francisco
> *The Serenity Principle: Finding Inner Peace in Recovery*
> Harper San Francisco

Marti Erickson, PhD
Parenting, child and family expert
E-mail: marti@momenough.com
www.MomEnough.com is a website where you can find the weekly talk show, Mom Enough™, hosted by developmental psychologist Dr. Marti Erickson and her daughter Erin Erickson, maternal-child health specialist. The site also includes links to TV appearances by Marti and Erin, as well as other print resources from Marti and Erin's work and that of their supporting partners.

Publications include:
Erickson, M. F., and K. Kurz-Riemer. *Infants, Toddlers and Families: A Framework for Support and Intervention.* New York: Guilford Publications, 2002.

Gaye Lindfors

Founder of Significant Solutions, Inc.
Strategic business consultant, career coach
Gaye@SignificantSolutionsInc.com
www.SignificantSolutionsInc.com
www.GayeLindfors.com
Author of *Find a Job: The Little Book for Big Success*
Contributing author to *Don't Miss Your Boat: Living Your Life with Purpose in the Real World*
Books can be purchased at www.GayeLindfors.com.

Linda Anderson

Cofounder of Angel Animals Network
www.angelanimals.net
angelanimals@aol.com
Coauthor of the Angel Animal series of books, including:
Angel Animals: Divine Messengers of Miracles
> *Angel Animals: Book of Inspiration: Divine Messengers of Wisdom and Compassion*
> *Rescued: Saving Animals from Disaster*
> *Dogs and the Women Who Love Them*

Kristine Greer

Founder and executive director of Charlene's Light, a foundation for women fighting ovarian cancer
Kristine Greer is passionate about reaching out and making a difference in the fight against ovarian cancer. If you would like more information or to invite Kristine to speak to your organization, please go to www.charleneslight.org.
krisgreer@yahoo.com

CPSIA information can be obtained at www.ICGtesting.com
Printed in the USA
BVOW070455291111

277115BV00003B/56/P

9 781452 539